D0312370

Praise for *The Customer Delight Principle*
by Timothy Keiningham and Terry Vavra

"For many years now, we at Harrah's have implemented measures, processes, and incentives that are based on the customer delight principles described by Keiningham and Vavra. Our employees know that growth and profitability rest with changes in customer behavior, not simply improvements in customer satisfaction. This book does a great job of first demonstrating this crucial distinction and then providing methods for instituting organizational reforms to take advantage of the enormous opportunity associated with enhanced customer loyalty."

—Gary W. Loveman, COO, Harrah's Entertainment, Inc.

"Whereas customer satisfaction is a ticket to play, customer delight is a ticket to survive. Through numerous illustrative examples Keiningham and Vavra document this fact plus provide guidance to success. My guess is that *The Customer Delight Principle* will soon establish itself as a must-read for those who want to attract and retain customers effectively."

—Professor Tor W. Andreassen, Norwegian School of Management

"A must-read for every entrepreneur who believes that success depends on satisfying the customer. *The Customer Delight Principle* shows how out-of-date customer satisfaction thinking is, and it does so with easily understood examples, stories, and numbers."

—Senator Feargal Quinn, CEO, Superquinn Stores, Ireland, and author of *Crowning the Customer: How to Become Customer-Driven*

"*The Customer Delight Principle* not only reinforces the need to break the service myth of customer satisfaction but also opens up a new Pandora's box in the services management field for the years to come."

—Professor Javier Reynoso, Services Management Research and Education Group, ITESM, Monterrey, Mexico

"Read this book before your competitors do! *The Customer Delight Principle* provides the framework and valuable insights for strategically delivering delight programs that build customer equity. It is crucial reading for any delight-seeking company interested in developing loyal relationships with high-value customers."

—Ed Routon, CEO, Alcott Routon, Inc.

"Finally someone has made the case to move from satisfaction to delight. Keiningham and Vavra have captured very clearly the two most fundamental requirements for creating a delight—a thorough understanding of customers' expectations and the commitment of business leaders. Companies who fail to make customer delight a part of their strategic business model will quickly be overrun by those who embrace this concept and make it an essential part of their daily lives. That means that not only organizations but also every department within them must understand the principles of what delights their customers and eliminate anything that causes pain—both internally and externally. I intend to make this book required reading for every leader in our organization."

    —Barbara Fitzgerald, Senior Vice President, PETsMART, Inc.

"I see many large organizations that go through the motions of customer satisfaction measurement (CSM) without really understanding why they are doing it or what they hope to gain from it. Some even question the value of this essential activity because they gain so little from it. Keiningham and Vavra neatly expose the problem in this very helpful book that every CSM manager should read. They clearly explain why a focus on merely satisfying customers is indeed unlikely to be a rewarding investment of the organization's resources. By using clearly detailed examples of the struggles of several real firms the authors provide clear and practical guidance about how to make CSM pay off."

    —Anthony Zahorik, Ph.D., Vice President, ACNielsen Burke Institute

"This book provides fact-loaded, real-life case studies that bring the customer delight principle vividly alive with no sugarcoating. It transcends dry, academic bookstore fare in a way that practitioners and others can embrace and use in their day-to-day jobs. At the same time, it offers quantitative tools that can be readily applied for those so inclined. The book is a virtual road map for companies and managers who seek to develop stronger linkages between customer delight and the bottom line. Outstanding!"

    —James A. Welch, Principal, Pittiglio Rabin Todd & McGrath

"Much has been written about customer satisfaction, a key challenge facing managers in today's global economy. Keiningham and Vavra's book, *The Customer Delight Principle*, is an enlightening work, rich in examples and offering a thorough, step-by-step guideline to be implemented in order to achieve the desired profitability associated with delighted customers. Their work certainly falls in the 'zone of delight'."

    —Josué Christiano Gomes da Silva, CEO, Coteminas,
    São Paulo, Brazil

/M\' AMERICAN **MARKETING** ASSOCIATION

THE
CUSTOMER
DELIGHT
PRINCIPLE

Exceeding Customers'
Expectations for
Bottom-Line Success

Timothy Keiningham and Terry Vavra

McGraw-Hill

Chicago   New York   San Francisco   Lisbon   London   Madrid   Mexico City
Milan   New Delhi   San Juan   Seoul   Singapore   Sydney   Toronto

Library of Congress Cataloging-in-Publication Data

Keiningham, Timothy L.
    The customer delight principle : exceeding customers' expectations for bottom-line success / Timothy L. Keiningham and Terry G. Vavra.
        p.   cm. (American Marketing Association).
    Includes index.
    ISBN 0-658-01004-2
    1. Consumer satisfaction.   2. Success in business.   I. Vavra, Terry G.
II. Title.

HF5415.335 .K45   2001
658.8'12—dc21   00-66217

McGraw-Hill

A Division of The **McGraw·Hill** *Companies*

1 2 3 4 5 6 7 8 9 0   LBM/LBM   0 9 8 7 6 5 4 3 2 1

ISBN 0-658-01004-2

This book was set in Sabon by Rattray Design
Printed and bound by Lake Book Manufacturing

This book is printed on acid-free paper.

To those who bring delight to our lives: our wives,
Michiko Keiningham and Linda Vavra;
and our children, Hana and Sage Keiningham and
Stacy (Roux), Kerry, and Tammy Vavra.

Contents

Preface

CUSTOMER SATISFACTION HAS become the mantra for success among companies throughout the industrialized world. Business enterprises, organizations, and institutions are all focused on measuring and improving the satisfaction of external and internal customers. The logic supporting this tactic is that customer satisfaction and customer retention move hand-in-hand, leading to improved market share and profits. Yet, numerous studies have shown that anywhere from 60 percent to 85 percent of customers who switch firms would have been classified as satisfied according to conventional analytic procedures. A contradiction? We believe the anomaly stems not from the basic precept that satisfying customers is a worthwhile endeavor but rather from the specific way satisfaction is measured and classified and exactly what happens (or doesn't happen) as a result of that information.

With *The Customer Delight Principle* we hope to alert the business community to the pitfalls of managing for improved satisfaction. While the relationships are far more complex than previously conceived, the rewards are no less compelling. Organizations that understand our principles and manage accordingly will succeed and handsomely so.

Satisfaction can be measured along a continuum. The three major points on this continuum are the Zone of Pain, the Zone of Mere Satisfaction, and the Zone of Delight. The Zone of Pain is the point in which a company is not satisfying its customers' needs. The Zone of

Mere Satisfaction is just past that point, in which the company is fulfilling needs but not doing much to distinguish itself from any other company within the same market. Most companies lie within the Zone of Mere Satisfaction. Success comes from moving customers beyond the relatively flat Zone of Mere Satisfaction to the point where customers demonstrate behaviors consistent with the goals of the firm (for example, increased retention, sales, word-of-mouth recommendations). This is the Zone of Delight. The term *delight* clearly delineates that mere satisfaction in today's market is not enough. This is what is meant by the customer delight principle.

Our goal in writing this book is to expose business leaders to a philosophy that we have proven to work. Our perspective uses current tools but imposes a more stringent way of applying decision rules. We also offer an evolutionary way of looking at the frequently misunderstood category of "key drivers." We believe that businesses that adopt our ideas can distinguish themselves as category leaders. Most of all, we hope our ideas will help overcome the apathy with which management reacts to so many current customer satisfaction programs.

Acknowledgments

SIR ISAAC NEWTON once wrote, "If I have seen further it is by standing on the shoulders of giants." Without question, if we have seen further, it is because of the influence of many gifted individuals.

It is impossible to thank all of the people who provided support in the writing of this book. However, several individuals and companies were invaluable to the completion of this book. We are especially thankful to all of the clients of Marketing Metrics, whose partnership has shaped our thinking and enriched our lives. We owe a special debt to Susan Boche, Monica Wood, Gerry Parker, and Ronda Senior of Toys "R" Us; Joe Steed, Harry Ryan, and Dave Schoenbeck of Babies "R" Us; Jim Scarfone, Jim Parros, Marcia Chiaverini, and Maureen Ksiez of Kids "R" Us; Andy Watt and Alasdair Stewart of Rolls-Royce and Bentley Motor Cars; Melinda Goddard of Roche Laboratories; Olga Striltschuk, Bob Pecho, and George Chemers of Motorola NSS; and Mark Juron, Maura Gallagher, Klaus Ulkan, Margret Diederle, Gail Fernandez, and Patti Durkin of Mercedes-Benz USA for their day-in, day-out commitment to the customer delight principle.

In addition, we want to thank the executives of the companies we have identified in this book, who generously contributed their time and insight through in-depth interviews for specific cases mentioned. These include R. Bruce Simpson, FedEx Custom Critical; Carlo Medici, Covance; Susan

Boche, Toys "R" Us; Joe Steed, Babies "R" Us; Mark Juron and Maura Gallagher, Mercedes-Benz USA.

We wish to thank all of our colleagues at Marketing Metrics, whose talent, imagination, and dedication are a fountain of inspiration. We especially want to thank Kenneth Peterson and Karen Liu for their review and contributions to a series of drafts as this book took shape, which greatly aided in the quality of the final manuscript.

The actual writing benefited from the contributions of several individuals. Gene Anderson and Vikas Mittal showed us how to decipher customer delight data and coauthored Chapter 4 with us. Roland Rust showed us how the new economy drives the customer delight principle and coauthored Chapter 5 with us.

We are indebted to our agent, Sally Wecksler, of Wecksler-Incomco, whose support and encouragement kept things moving along when the tasks seemed insurmountable.

We are grateful to Danielle Egan-Miller, Katherine Hinkebein, and Sybil Sosin at McGraw-Hill, whose comments on style and substance helped to transform our manuscript into something far more readable than we could have accomplished on our own.

Satisfaction Guaranteed

"YOUR SATISFACTION IS guaranteed." The phrase is ubiquitous—almost cliche. Whether it be expensive office equipment, a hotel stay, or a bag of cheese puffs, it is almost certain that "your total satisfaction is guaranteed or your money back." The reason is self-evident: Dissatisfied customers are bad for business. They don't come back. And all too often, they tell their friends why. As a result, the quest for 100 percent satisfaction has become a strategic imperative for many firms. Consequently, the popularity of customer satisfaction programs has soared. The conventional logic is simple enough to understand: If *dissatisfied* customers are bad for business, then *satisfied* customers must be good for business.

Overwhelming scientific evidence supports management's focus on customer satisfaction. In particular, researchers have found that firms that create superior customer satisfaction enjoy superior profits. Researchers from the University of Michigan found that, on average, every 1 percent increase in customer satisfaction is associated with a 2.37 percent increase in a firm's Return on Investment (ROI). And without a doubt, there are a lot of success stories—perhaps none better than that of FedEx Custom Critical (formerly Roberts Express).

The Ubiquity of Satisfaction Promises

- "I'm listening."
  —Gordon Bethune, CEO, Continental Airlines

- "Customers' safety and satisfaction are our No. 1 concerns."
  —Masatoshi Ono, CEO, Bridgestone/Firestone

- "I'm out there every day spending 60 percent of my time with customers just to set an example."
  —Tom Siebel, CEO, Siebel Systems

- "If a customer says that he or she is dissatisfied, that's good enough for us."
  —Tom Jones, President and CEO, StrataSource

King of the Road

FedEx Custom Critical was formed in 1948 through the merger of two Ohio trucking companies. Throughout most of its early history, it was a regional transporter of airfreight, first for the airlines and later for Emery Air Freight. In 1981, seeing an untapped opportunity for a high-performance, surface-based alternative to airfreight, the company became the first to specialize in expedited, door-to-door shipment of critical items. That first year sales were just over $2 million, but growth in subsequent years was exponential. By 1990 the company was the largest at-the-moment surface expedited carrier.

Stellar growth came with a price. R. Bruce Simpson, president of FedEx Custom Critical, became increasingly troubled by what he was reading in his monthly customer satisfaction reports. Although the satisfaction scores were good, clients began complaining that the company had become too large and bureaucratic. "They were saying, 'I'm calling a customer service organization and one of a hundred people could pick up the phone,'" says Simpson.

Simpson knew many of these customers personally. Before becoming president in 1988, he had been manager of sales for the company. He knew firsthand the intimacy the company had enjoyed with its customers. As president, he had adopted customer satisfaction as a primary management tool. It became his passion if not his obsession. Every month, 150 recent customers were surveyed at random, and Simpson read *every* survey.

Early in 1991, in reviewing questionnaires, Simpson was confronted with a recurring theme: "You're getting too big. I'm losing my identity with you!" Simpson trusted and valued his customers; he responded to these complaints by shrinking the company. He divided operations into self-managed Customer Assistance Teams (CAT). Each CAT was assigned to a specific geographic area. The result? To regular customers, FedEx Custom Critical is no bigger than the CAT that serves them. "It took three years to fully implement CAT, but we knew early on that the program would be a success," notes Simpson. "We had measures in place to gauge customer satisfaction, and we found that the customers and the drivers were more satisfied with CAT than with the system it replaced, and morale went up accordingly."

FedEx Custom Critical also facilitated customer intimacy through its information technology. The telephone system was set up to route calls to the appropriate CAT. If a customer made more than one call on the same day, that customer was automatically routed to the same dispatcher he or she spoke with earlier. The telephone system was also set up to search a database containing hundreds of thousands of customers. If a match was found, a pop-up window appeared on the dispatcher's computer screen providing a detailed profile of the incalling customer, all before the phone was picked up.

"We knew from our customer surveys that in most cases customers are calling us in an emergency, and they want to get off the phone as quickly as possible so they can go back to handling the crisis," says Joel Childs, vice president of marketing. "By having the customer's information readily available on our team member's computer screen, we can skip over basic information such as name and phone number and go right to the important issues in setting up the shipment. That makes us more productive, and it pleases our customers."

Nothing is more important than satisfying the customer, and at FedEx Custom Critical they are very satisfied. Through his response, Simpson successfully corrected any detriment the 1991 comments might have foretold. Year after year, in excess of 90 percent of customers surveyed rated their experience at the very highest level on the company's customer satisfaction survey (see Figure 1.1). Likewise, growth has con-

Figure 1.1 FedEx Custom Critical Customer "Top-Box"
Satisfaction Levels (1988–1999)

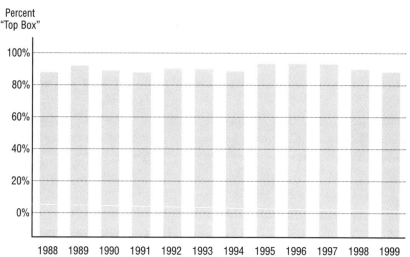

Source: FedEx Custom Critical (formerly Roberts Express).

tinued to soar, no doubt in large part because of the high level of satisfaction. Since becoming president in 1988, Simpson has watched North American revenues more than quadruple, achieving a compounded annual growth rate of almost 14 percent. (These figures would be even higher if international expansion were included!)

Simpson is committed to making certain that this fortunate picture never changes. The company is obsessed with measuring performance. The feedback from the satisfaction survey is reported throughout the entire organization. In the center of each CAT station stands a board that tells everyone how the teams are doing. There's more at stake than team pride. Each team member's quarterly bonus is tied to these numbers. In fact, Simpson estimates that half of the employees and managers, including Simpson himself, have measurable objectives defined in the company's Management by Objectives (MBO) system. Fulfillment of these objectives, which is tied directly to customer satisfaction levels, determines quarterly bonuses.

In addition, all employees at FedEx Custom Critical participate in a gain-sharing plan, wherein everyone, regardless of position, receives an equal annual bonus that is tied to the results of the customer satisfaction survey. "I [convinced] the chairman of the board that we wanted to do

---

CASE CRITIQUE

FedEx Custom Critical

- Success was based on personal touch, knowing customers' needs, and setting a goal of delighting customers.

- With fast growth, the customers' identities and preferences were becoming lost; delight was changing to mere satisfaction.

- The CEO heard customers' complaints and reorganized the company around the customer—each customer was assigned to a small Customer Assistance Team (CAT).

- Rather than allowing the technology that comes with size to further distance the company from its customers, technology was used to regain the personal touch, providing each CAT with seamless status reports on customers' shipments and preferences.

---

something to compensate the performance of our people, collectively, over the year, after achieving a certain level of profitability," explains Simpson. "Beyond that [level of profit], we put 20 percent into a pot, and depending upon customer satisfaction for the whole year, we'll pay anywhere from 50 percent to 100 percent of that money." Last year, that amounted to about $6,000 to every full-time employee.

The satisfaction measurement and incentive process doesn't end there. Departments whose function is to support the employees of FedEx Custom Critical, such as information technology and human resources, survey their "internal customers" on a quarterly basis. The results of these surveys determine quarterly bonuses for members of these departments.

In addition, every eighteen months employees are surveyed to measure their morale. And every quarter random surveys are conducted among the company's drivers, who are independent contractors, not employees. Drivers represent the company's most important suppliers, and they have direct contact with the customer. FedEx Custom Critical has been able to maintain one of the lowest driver turnover rates in the industry.

Simpson proudly notes that Fred Smith, CEO of parent company FedEx, has called FedEx Custom Critical the crown jewel of the FedEx system. "Everybody talks about customer satisfaction, but few companies measure it and even fewer implement it," observes Simpson. "I feel as if what I'm saying is so obvious, but it seems to me that it's still something that isn't done by everyone."

FedEx Custom Critical exemplifies the best-case scenario for firms that embark on a customer satisfaction strategy. Superior customer satisfaction leads to customer retention, market share, and profits.

Unfortunately, success is not universal. What seems so intuitive to some has proved difficult for other managers to apply to their firms. In the case of First American Bank, instead of satisfaction making this company "king of the road," the consequence was more like roadkill.

Roadkill

Kenneth L. Roberts was the epitome of a bank CEO—an imposing six-foot, five-inch frame with graying hair and shrouded in a blue pinstripe suit. He was also one of the most recognizable bankers in the state of Tennessee, known to thousands who had never personally met him or even visited a First American Bank branch office. He appeared in countless local television commercials as the spokesman for the bank. Whether he was dismissing the importance of computerization while standing in front of a profusion of computer hardware or simply discussing the merits of First American's services, his basic message was always the same: At First American, "Banking is a people business!"

New Competition

Roberts's focus on the people aspects of banking was no accident. In the mid-1980s First American found itself in uncharted waters. Competition was emerging from a host of new sources, siphoning off business by offering many traditional banking services. Customers could suddenly write checks on money market funds arranged through their brokers, purchase annuities through their insurance agents, and finance their automobiles through the manufacturers. In essence, banks found themselves being cherry-picked of some of their more profitable services.

At the same time, legislation allowing interstate banking loomed on the horizon as a foregone conclusion. Large national and regional banks would be able to go head-to-head with competitors throughout the country. And larger banks had a significant advantage over their smaller rivals since they could spread their costs over higher transaction volumes. The rise of interstate banking combined with a general overcapacity in the industry guaranteed consolidation, meaning many smaller banks would find themselves swallowed up by larger institutions.

While First American Corporation was the second largest bank-holding company in Tennessee, with 150 branches, 4,000 employees, and more than $7 billion in assets, it was substantially smaller than either its national or regional competitors. It wasn't a technology leader, either, having no branch automation system in place. If First American were going to survive, it would have to find a way to effectively compete against its more cost-efficient competitors. CEO Roberts and his officers decided that the way to compete would be through high-quality service—that is, through higher customer satisfaction with First American relative to its competitors.

Monitoring the Strategy

By 1989 First American was surveying more than 11,000 of its customers, asking them to rate their satisfaction with twenty-two separate service-quality characteristics. In addition to measuring customers' overall satisfaction with the corporation and with individual branches, the survey sought to determine customers' willingness to recommend the bank to others and their intention of increasing business with First American. Not surprisingly, there was a direct correlation between customers' overall satisfaction levels and their stated likelihood of increasing business with First American or of recommending the bank to others.

Every branch and district was held accountable for the performance on each of these twenty-two characteristics. Using the survey data, a performance matrix was created to identify areas of customer service in need of improvement.

So pervasive was the customer-survey process within First American that even branch employees were surveyed to determine their satisfaction with the performance of their fellow employees in the operations and information services group. Branch employees were asked their satisfaction concerning more than a hundred performance variables, ranging from the courtesy of the data-processing staff to the response time of on-line transactions to the quality of the local telephone company service. First American employees in the operations group that failed to "make the grade" were required to contact the branch that was dissatisfied and analyze how service might be improved.

While the mantra that "banking is a people business" most certainly reflected the ideals of Kenneth Roberts, First American's strategy was not simply altruistic. It was expected to demonstrate that it is good business to be good. As one First American vice president noted:

> By creating a quality program with a foundation based on customer perceptions and customer-sensitive issues, and backing it up with sound, quantifiable measurements, we have made a genuine commitment to superior quality and excellence. Our ultimate success depends on it. This is our goal and mission at First American and we are all committed to it. In the long run this will be a quality program we can all "bank" on.

On Strategy, Off Profitability

Unfortunately for First American, the road to profitability through superior customer satisfaction was anything but smooth. By 1990 First American found itself awash in red ink, with bad loans costing the bank $60 million. The loss was so significant that federal banking regulators from the Federal Reserve, the Federal Deposit Insurance Company (FDIC), and the Office of the Comptroller of the Currency (OCC) met with members of the board. To quote one person familiar with the meetings, "They were highly critical of the bank's performance" and discussed the bank's leadership. As a result, on March 29, 1990, Roberts was fired as chairman, CEO, and president by First American Corporation's bank board.

Almost immediately, the strategy at First American changed. The headline from a 1991 article in the periodical *Bank Letter* seems to say it all: "Individual Bank Strategies: First American Pushes for Cost Containment." First American downsized its staff from 4,000 to 3,300. The bank also strengthened lending requirements, centralized its underwriting process to reduce expenditures, began evaluating employee productivity, and restructured its branch operations to enhance sales. Furthermore, First American upgraded its technology through a then-unusual agreement with IBM. Not only would IBM take over First American's back-office processing, but it would also install a customized branch automation system. The outsourcing arrangement with IBM was expected to cut $40 million in costs for First American over ten years.

CASE CRITIQUE

First American Bank

- When developing and implementing its service strategy, First American failed to focus on the core drivers of profitability in its industry (i.e., loan quality, fee income, and the interest spread realized between the payment for deposits and revenue from loans).

- Technology was not used to improve customer intimacy, improve efficiency, or reduce service costs.

- Customer service levels were not tied to individual customer profitability or potential profitability.

- Operating costs outpaced requisite profits.

Almost as quickly as First American changed its focus to cost containment did its fortunes change. By 1991 First American was in the black, with rising earnings in subsequent years (see Figure 1.2).

The Siren's Call

First American Corporation's attempt to compete for superior customer satisfaction with its service was by no means an unpopular strategy in the banking industry at the time. The Bank Marketing Association (BMA) and its affiliated trade journal *Bank Marketing* were replete with exhortations for banks to compete on service.

- "Service quality is shaping up as the marketing imperative of the '90s. . . . Service quality has become one of the few areas in which banks can differentiate themselves."   —Mary Colby, associate editor, *Bank Marketing* magazine

Figure 1.2 First American Net Income

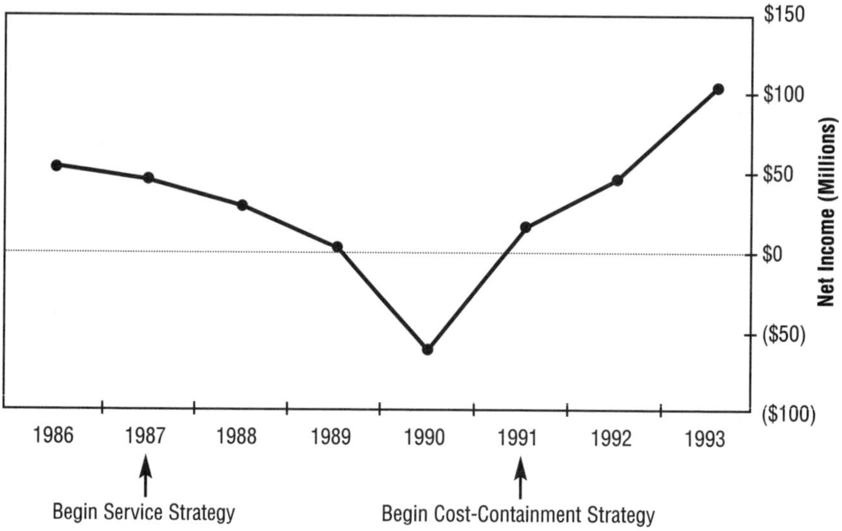

Begin Service Strategy

Begin Cost-Containment Strategy

Source: Annual Reports.

• "Quality is America's greatest challenge. . . . The lesson needs to be applied to banking as well." —J. Douglas Adamson, executive vice president and chief executive officer, Bank Marketing Association of Chicago

Between 1987 and 1992, nearly one hundred articles in *Bank Marketing* discussed the importance of customer satisfaction and service quality in banking. So convinced was the BMA that in 1989 it established the Quality Focus Institute for the study and improvement of service-quality management in the financial-services industry. The institute was chartered to "provide education, research, and other support to financial institutions seeking to improve their service quality."

In order to determine the current state of service quality in banks and where they should focus their improvement efforts, the Quality Focus Institute offered Service Quality Satisfaction Analysis (SQSA). In essence, the Institute would survey a bank's customers, calculate a bank's current satisfaction level, and from this information produce a strategy map to identify the appropriate course of action. In addition to individual bank studies, the Quality Focus Institute conducted national studies of customer satisfaction using the SQSA methodology. The BMA heralded the first national study as a means for banks to gauge their performance levels versus national norms:

> The BMA's Quality Focus Institute will announce the results of the first National Consumer Study of Service Quality in Banking. This benchmark study, based on the Institute's survey of 23,000 consumers nationally, will spotlight key areas of customer satisfaction and dissatisfaction. By conducting this study annually, the Quality Focus Institute will establish national levels of customer satisfaction against which banks can compare their own measurements. In tandem with Service Quality Satisfaction Analysis (SQSA) . . . this information will help banks across the country gauge their own customer satisfaction levels in terms of national and regional norms.

The expressed promise was that service quality is a "strategic management process that affects every aspect of financial-services marketing—and produces real, quantifiable benefits . . . [including] greater customer satisfaction and retention; better resource allocation; lower operating costs; [and] increased opportunities for value-added pricing." And the means for gathering the marketing intelligence necessary for success was Service Quality Satisfaction Analysis.

Unfortunately, many financial institutions found that the promise of greater profits was elusive. They were so elusive, in fact, that the Council on Financial Competition, a strategic research firm and for-profit think tank targeting the banking industry, staked out what was at the time a self-acknowledged "contrarian" position in its first overview of the state of service quality in the banking industry:

> Service quality as an issue is seriously overrated; service certainly is not as important as the mythic proportions it has taken on in industry trade publications and conferences. While service quality is a burning issue for financial firms, it emphatically is not for most consumers; in recent research, 92 percent of consumers polled rated their banking service "good" or "excellent." Only 3 percent judged the level of service provided to them as "poor." Moreover, it is clear that very few customers of that very small minority unhappy about service quality actually leave the institution over the issue. On the average, only 10 percent to 15 percent of closed accounts can be attributed to service problems.

The council's position ultimately became the prevailing viewpoint. Continued lack of returns by banks seeking to differentiate themselves through customer satisfaction and service quality led to increasing skepticism. Faced with an increasingly disillusioned membership, the Bank Marketing Association discontinued the Service Quality Satisfaction Analysis and ultimately dissolved its Quality Focus Institute.

The Uncertainty Principle

Unfortunately, such disturbing scenarios are not limited to the banking industry. All too often customer satisfaction results appear to be completely disconnected from business performance. Take, for example, the hotel industry. Frequently confronted with time-consuming check-ins, "bumped" reservations, erratic wake-up calls, and poor housekeeping, the lodging industry has received a crush of complaints from business and leisure travelers. Adding insult to injury, the dimensions of the rooms at some of the most prestigious hotels have shrunk to near broom-closet size, while their prices have skyrocketed. Not surprisingly, approximately 22 percent of customers surveyed for the 1998 American Customer Satisfaction Index (ACSI) voiced complaints about their hotel stays. The industry has watched its customer satisfaction levels drop to unprecedented lows. Over the same time period, however, the hotel industry has posted record profits (see Figure 1.3).

Similar observations can be made for companies in a variety of industries. Wal-Mart Corporation, Southwest Airlines, and Colgate Palmolive

Figure 1.3 *Customer Satisfaction and Profitability in the Hotel/Motel Industry*

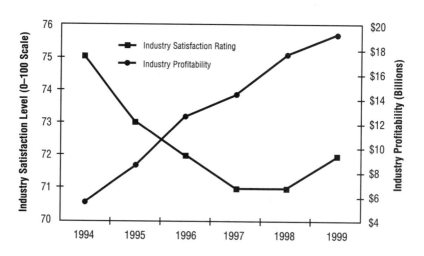

Sources: American Customer Satisfaction Index (produced through a partnership with the University of Michigan Business School, American Society for Quality, and Arthur Andersen); Malley, Mike (1997). "Lodging Industry Stays on Efficient Course: STR Chapter 1—Figures Tell the Story," Hotel and Motel Management. 212 (October 20): 1; and Business Wire (1998). "Fears of Overbuilding Are Overblown, Lodging Research Network Says," Business Wire (July 6).

have all seen their ACSI scores drop while their net incomes have risen to record levels (see Figures 1.4a, 1.4b, and 1.4c). Such anomalies can cast doubt on the value of improving customer satisfaction even among satisfaction's staunchest allies.

An Implementation Problem

These examples clearly demonstrate that the link between customer satisfaction and profit is not a simple equation; satisfaction doesn't guarantee profits and sometimes profits occur in the absence of satisfaction. The failure of customer satisfaction initiatives to produce measurable results has provoked many people to openly challenge the value of such efforts. Some have labeled satisfaction measurement a trap in the pursuit of customer loyalty. Books with titles such as *Customer Satisfaction Is Worthless, Customer Loyalty Is Priceless* and *Beyond Customer Satisfaction to Customer Loyalty: The Key to Greater Profitability* have capitalized on the disillusionment many managers have with customer

Figure 1.4a *Customer Satisfaction and Profitability for Wal-Mart*

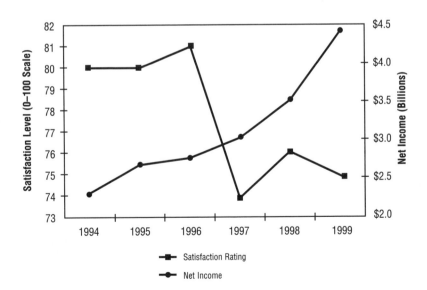

Sources: American Customer Satisfaction Index (produced through a partnership with the University of Michigan Business School, American Society for Quality, and Arthur Andersen); Annual Reports.

Figure 1.4b *Customer Satisfaction and Profitability for Southwest Airlines*

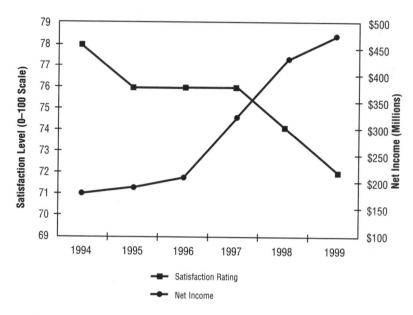

Sources: *American Customer Satisfaction Index (produced through a partnership with the University of Michigan Business School, American Society for Quality, and Arthur Andersen); Annual Reports.*

satisfaction as a means for optimizing profitability. However, we believe listening to the skeptics is a mistake. While there is no question that many customer satisfaction initiatives fail, the failure is not the fault of the underlying strategy. Rather, the failure is a result of poor implementation. Specifically, most programs fail because managers don't comprehend or appreciate the nature of the impact of customer satisfaction on financial performance.

So how come what worked so well for FedEx Custom Critical didn't have a similar outcome for the vast majority of financial institutions? A clue to the underlying difference lies in the stated mission of FedEx Custom Critical: "We will delight our customers worldwide by providing fast, precise, dedicated transportation services. We will provide personal service and will be the best at doing this, guaranteed. Our primary measurement will be the customer perception of satisfaction."

"We will delight our customers!" That is quite different from, "Your satisfaction is guaranteed." "Satisfaction guaranteed" simply commits the

Figure 1.4c *Customer Satisfaction and Profitability for Colgate Palmolive*

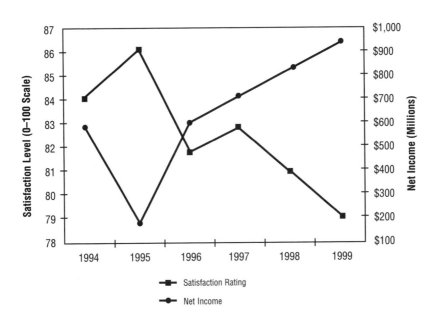

Sources: American Customer Satisfaction Index (produced through a partnership with the University of Michigan Business School, American Society for Quality, and Arthur Andersen); Annual Reports.

firm to preventing *dis*satisfaction. "Delight," on the other hand, commits a firm to attaining the very highest level of customer satisfaction.

Not a Straight Line

Oftentimes managers don't realize that the impact of an increase in customer satisfaction levels is almost never as substantial as an equivalent decrease in satisfaction. Some processes are negatively biased, meaning that a decrease in average satisfaction levels will have a greater impact than an equivalent increase. For others, gains in satisfaction will have greater impact than will declines.

Adding to the difficulty, the relationship between satisfaction and customer behavior is not linear. At some points the relationship shows diminishing returns. In other words, each consecutive and equivalently sized increase in average satisfaction levels will have a smaller impact on behavior than the preceding increase. Likewise, at other points there are increasing returns. Failure to recognize the nature of satisfaction makes it virtually impossible to correctly prioritize improvement efforts. Consequently, achieving profitability through improved satisfaction has frequently been as much a matter of luck as of science.

Recent studies show there are thresholds of satisfaction beyond which little benefit is obtained (see Figure 1.5). As a company reaches customers' minimally acceptable satisfaction level, it becomes a viable alternative for customers' consideration. In short, the company is providing the bare necessities and is therefore "in the game." Once at that point, however, there is a discontinuity in the relationship between satisfaction and customer behavior. We refer to this transition point as moving from the Zone of Pain to the Zone of Mere Satisfaction.

Falling into the Zone of Pain is a reliable predictor of customer defection. A company cannot survive in this region, unless its strategy is pure price leadership and customers are willing to trade off satisfaction for a

Figure 1.5 *Impact of Satisfaction and Delight*

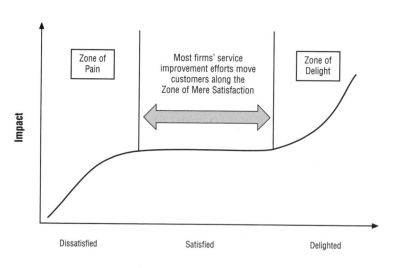

Level of Customer Satisfaction

Adapted from: Rust, Roland T., Anthony J. Zahorik, and Timothy L. Keiningham (1994). Return on Quality: Measuring the Financial Impact of Your Company's Quest for Quality. New York: McGraw-Hill Irwin. Reproduced with permission of The McGraw-Hill Companies.

Why Satisfaction Isn't a Panacea

- Merely satisfying one's customers is a low hurdle—you should aim for delight.

- Understanding how customer satisfaction translates into retention, increased market share, and enhanced profitability is key.

- Satisfaction isn't an end in itself—it triggers a chain of results. Astute managers will strive to better understand that chain before investing in it.

---

low price. For most companies, this is not a winning situation—mere satisfaction seldom drives profits. While failure on some processes will certainly create dissatisfaction and cause customers to leave, customers take success in these same areas for granted. For example, if a bank incorrectly processed checks, it would most certainly dissatisfy its customers and lose market share. But not bouncing customers' checks would hardly offer the bank a point of competitive differentiation.

Summary

Most firms provide the necessities customers require of them. If they didn't, they wouldn't be in business (or remain in business for long). As a result, the vast majority of firms do not have a groundswell of dissatisfied customers. Instead, most businesses have customers who can be classified as satisfied with their overall experience with the business. Unfortunately, moving customers along the "merely satisfied" section of the satisfaction continuum rarely provides a positive impact. It is in this Zone of Mere Satisfaction that the relationship between customer satisfaction and customer behavior appears to break down. Therefore, improvement efforts that result in only small improvements in satisfaction levels tend to be unprofitable.

Managers have discovered to their dismay that 60 percent of customers who leave to find another firm or brand would classify themselves as "satisfied." This isn't surprising, however, considering that virtually all firms deliver the necessities—slight differences in mere satisfaction levels are unlikely to engender loyalty.

Instead, success comes when customers move beyond the Zone of Mere Satisfaction and onto the point where they will demonstrate behaviors consistent with the goals of the firm. This is called the Zone of Delight. To achieve remarkable success in a category, customers need to be able to describe their experience as delightful. In such cases, customers will remain loyal, will help attract other customers, and will increase their spending levels. It is at this point that generating satisfaction really pays dividends.

Clearly, Simpson of FedEx Custom Critical recognized his opportunity to exceed customers' expectations and thereby delight them. While he needed to invest to enable his strategy, he was convinced that his investment would be paid back, based on its relevance to the customers and the customers' economic value to the firm. His strategy has been rewarded by substantial loyalty and substantial profitability. On the other hand, despite great hoopla, the majority of financial institutions in the 1990s found that the promise of greater profits through improved customer satisfaction were illusive. For most, the goals were too modest; the resulting revenue couldn't begin to pay back the costs involved.

Managers who recognize the value of the customer delight principle not only avoid underestimating the importance of customer satisfaction but actually profit from it. The objective must be to move customers up the satisfaction continuum from the Zone of Mere Satisfaction to the Zone of Delight, and keep them there. To quote R. Bruce Simpson, CEO of FedEx Custom Critical, "The strategy for us is to absolutely delight the customers."

Chapter Key Notes

- While many firms have adopted a goal of 100 percent satisfaction, merely satisfying customers is no guarantee of success.
- The failure of firms to achieve financial results from their satisfaction initiatives has caused many to question the value of such efforts.

- Failure is largely caused by a lack of understanding of the nature of the relationship between satisfaction and customer behavior. In particular, there are different thresholds of satisfaction, which we refer to as the Zone of Pain, the Zone of Mere Satisfaction, and the Zone of Delight.
- Success comes when customers are moved out of the Zone of Mere Satisfaction and into the Zone of Delight.

Zone Defense: Pain, Satisfaction, and Delight

MIRAGE. DELUSION. Hallucination. Illusion. Fantasy. Our language is replete with words to describe a mistaken perception of reality. But for managers, customers' perceptions are every bit as important as reality. In fact, it matters little if so-called objective measures indicate a certain condition if customers perceive something else to be the case. To your customers, their perception is their reality.

Unfortunately, customers' perceptions can be absolutely inaccurate, a great source of frustration for managers. Take the following examples:

- The Chrysler Laser and the Mitsubishi Eclipse were virtually identical automobiles in all but the most superficial variations in trim. They were actually made at the same plant. But customers consistently rated the quality of the Chrysler version lower. And on a dealer-by-dealer basis, the Eclipse outsold the Laser by a ratio of 8 to 1.
- Parents in the United States consistently express high levels of satisfaction with their childcare facilities. But research conducted by four different universities in the mid-1990s found that only 15 percent could be classified as "excellent." The bottom 15 percent were "abysmal" and the middle 70 percent were "barely adequate."

Perceptions tend to generate emotional responses from customers. So managers must be concerned not only with how customers perceive service but also how they feel about it.

Can't Get No Satisfaction

If the American music channel VH1 is correct, then the Rolling Stones' "Satisfaction" is the greatest rock song ever. Whether this accolade is correct is debatable, but there can be no doubt that the lament punched out in the lyrics struck a chord with many: "I try and I try and I try and I try . . . I can't get no satisfaction."

But what exactly is satisfaction? The word *satisfaction* is derived from the Latin words *satis* and *facere*, which translate to mean "to make or do enough." This suggests that the true meaning of satisfaction is the fulfillment of needs, expectations, wishes, or desires. But to what extent? There are, naturally, gradations of satisfaction. Most typically, managers have sought to solve customers' problems as the primary way of satisfying them. But simply solving problems achieves only a minimally acceptable level of satisfaction, what we refer to as Mere Satisfaction. It is similar to thinking of something as adequate rather than exceptional. Quality guru W. Edwards Deming noted this possible trap, observing that "it will not suffice to have customers who are merely satisfied." A simple "no problem" approach to customer satisfaction is too limiting.

Professor Richard Oliver proposes a more extensive definition of customer satisfaction:

> Satisfaction is the consumer's fulfillment response. It is a judgment that a product or service feature, or the product or service itself, provided (or is providing) a pleasurable level of consumption-related fulfillment, including levels of under- or overfulfillment.

States of Satisfaction

Oliver's definition implies three general levels of fulfillment: underfulfillment, fulfillment, and overfulfillment. Underfulfillment corresponds to customer dissatisfaction, while fulfillment corresponds to mere satisfaction. The distinction between these two levels of satisfaction is whether or not customers believe what they are offered is adequate to fulfill their needs. Being adequate means that minimally acceptable thresholds are met on all characteristics that customers require from a product or service experience. As noted earlier, managerially this corresponds to preventing or solving customers' problems.

We refer to the state of dissatisfaction as the Zone of Pain. It is at this point that customers' needs are not being met on attributes that they believe the firm must have in order to be in business. As such, customers experience some degree of distress because of their disappointment with the unfulfilled-need experience. We refer to the area where must-have needs are adequately met as the Zone of Mere Satisfaction (see Figure 1.5 in Chapter 1).

Simply not experiencing pain, however, is not the highest level of satisfaction. No one would describe a true love as "adequately meeting my minimum needs." Going beyond mere satisfaction requires more than eliminating problems. It involves the concept of customer delight.

Delight

Recently both researchers and practitioners have begun to theorize that the levels beyond mere satisfaction can result in significantly better behavioral outcomes (such as customer retention, word-of-mouth recommendations, and share-of-wallet), which therefore have important financial implications for businesses. Within the Zone of Mere Satisfaction, differences between firms with regard to customer satisfaction do not produce much change in customer behavior and therefore in business results. Moving satisfaction scores beyond the upper threshold of this zone into customer delight, however, will create exceptional results. For many companies, customer delight has become a strategic imperative, as is illustrated through comments made by these CEOs:

- "Only when we were able to link quality-process means to the customer delight end were we finally able to integrate TQM (total quality management) into our culture." —Michael Bonsignore, CEO, Honeywell Inc.

- "Going *beyond* satisfaction to customer delight will provide a distinct advantage to the company that does it first and does it well consistently." —Colby H. Chandler, former chairman and CEO, Eastman Kodak

- "To really maximize the resources of the company, people have to know what's going on . . . with scoreboards letting folks know exactly how we're doing from our revenue growth standpoint, our profit growth standpoint, our customer delight standpoint, so our people know what's happening. It's critical." —Jerre Stead, CEO, Ingram Micro (former CEO, Legent Corporation)

- "To remind our employees that customer satisfaction isn't good enough, we substitute the phrase 'customer delight.' Delight is much more than service, support, or satisfaction." —Gilbert Amelio, president, AmTech, LLC (former CEO, Apple Computer and former CEO, National Semiconductor Corporation)

Even the comic-strip character Dilbert's rather thick-skulled boss has almost begun to get the message.

Despite the increasing managerial emphasis on the benefits of customer delight, there is no universal definition of what delight means. Academics tend to define delight in terms of "positive surprise." For example, delight has been defined as "an extreme expression of positive effect resulting from surprisingly good performance." Managers tend to define delight more pragmatically: "going beyond satisfaction," or perhaps, "exceeding customers' expectations." These definitions imply that, while

Used with permission of United Feature Syndicate, Inc.

Definitions of Customer Delight

- Positive surprise arising from extremely good service delivery or product performance
- The highest level of satisfaction
- Exceeding customers' expectations

---

a state of satisfaction may be induced by solving problems, creating delight requires more.

Our definition of delight corresponds to the managerial definition: Customer delight will only be achieved by exceeding all base expectations in the performance of a product or in the delivery of a service (or in the servicing that accompanies a product or service). Delight is the emotional response to an otherwise functional business transaction.

While there is no doubt that positive surprise will induce delight, consistently surprising customers is unlikely to be a viable business strategy for all but the most high-entertainment, limited-use businesses (such as theme parks, theaters, and the like). Simply put, it is difficult to be surprised by the familiar. This, however, does not mean that strong emotional responses cannot be obtained without surprise—quite the contrary.

Ample evidence supports the theory that behavioral benefits develop as a result of moving customers beyond the Zone of Mere Satisfaction. For example, researchers found that for Xerox, "totally satisfied" customers were six times more likely to repurchase Xerox products over the next eighteen months than customers who rated themselves as "satisfied."

Consistently delivering delight on differentiating attributes creates loyal behavior that cannot be achieved through mere satisfaction alone. This brings us to an additional component of our definition of delight: for customer delight to be relevant, it must be identifiable through its positive relationship with customer behavior. This marks a strong break with the academic definition. While it is possible to delight customers in the psychological sense without there being repeat-purchase behavior, as with unique vacations or theater productions, for managers, satisfaction and delight matter only to the extent that they impact customer behavior. As the purpose of this book is to maximize the impact of customer delight measurement and management, our use of the term *delight* will follow this narrower definition.

Uncertainty and Choice

As customers move along the satisfaction continuum from dissatisfaction to mere satisfaction to delight, the number of competitive alternatives they consider decreases accordingly (see Figure 2.1). Because movement through the Zone of Mere Satisfaction does not ordinarily result in large shifts in the number of competitors considered by customers, small changes in satisfaction levels in this area seldom have much impact.

This relationship can be explained in part by the role of uncertainty in customers' decisions. Figure 2.2 shows two customers' expectations of a particular outcome. The greater the experience level of the customer, the less uncertainty there is about what to expect from the experience. This is crucial because risk plays an important role in customers' decision making. People tend to be more averse to experiencing negative outcomes than they are willing to actively seek positive outcomes. From

Figure 2.1 *Impact of Satisfaction on the Number of Competitors Considered by Customers*

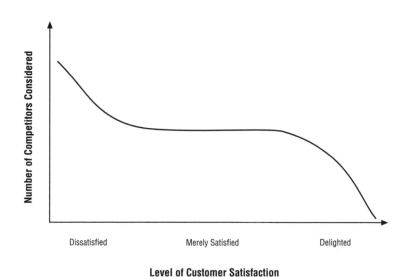

Figure 2.2 *Uncertainty in Expectations*

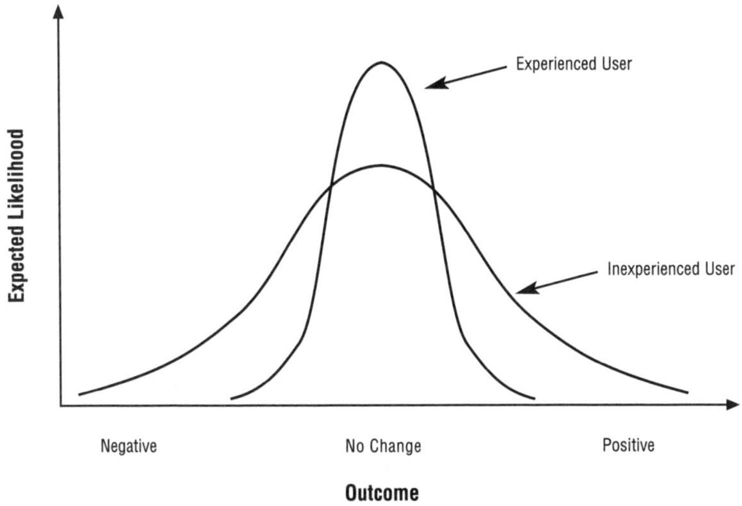

Adapted from: Rust, Roland T., Anthony J. Zahorik, and Timothy L. Keiningham (1994). Return on Quality: Measuring the Financial Impact of Your Company's Quest for Quality. New York: McGraw-Hill Irwin. Reproduced with permission of The McGraw-Hill Companies.

a business perspective this suggests that bad outcomes can hurt more than positive outcomes help.

It is not until customers perceive that certain thresholds will be reached that the potential upside of switching to a competitor outweighs the potential downside. For example, if a customer expects only a 50 percent chance of receiving better quality from a competitor, and the possibility of experiencing a bad outcome carries more weight in the customer's mind, it would be irrational for that customer to switch firms (see Figure 2.3). Therefore, it is perfectly rational for merely satisfied customers to remain with their firms if they perceive only a slightly greater likelihood of receiving better services or products from competitors. They are simply avoiding downside risk.

The Role of Expectations

Satisfaction and delight are strongly influenced by customers' expectations in regard to how the experience could, should, will, and better not occur.

Figure 2.3 *Expected Likelihood of Receiving a Better Experience from Competition Based on Current Level of Satisfaction*

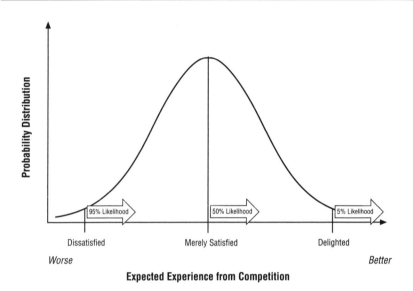

Note: Likelihood percentages are used for illustrative purposes only.

What customers believe will happen is the expectation level most often used by customers (and researchers). It is the level of quality customers predict they will receive.

But customers may also believe that what they will receive is not what they should receive. Frequently, what customers believe *should* happen is better than what they believe *will* happen. For example, many customers expect to deal with bureaucratic red tape when interacting with government agencies, but few believe that this should be the case.

The ideal expectation is what customers believe could happen in a best-case scenario. As such, it serves as a useful benchmark for excellence. On the lower end of the scale is the minimally acceptable level. The minimally acceptable level is the point that separates the Zone of Pain from the Zone of Mere Satisfaction. Below the minimally acceptable level is the worst possible level, the worst outcome imaginable (see Figure 2.4).

The difference between what customers expect to receive and what customers actually experience according to their perception is a very

---

Example of the Range of Expectations: Checking into a Hotel

- *Could*: Recognize me as a previous guest and thank me for returning, offering a courtesy upgrade to show appreciation

- *Should*: Have my reservation at hand, recognizing my frequent guest status and providing the accommodations I requested

- *Will*: Have a room available with the accommodations I've requested

- *Better Not*: Be oversold and either send me to another hotel or offer me a substandard room

---

strong predictor of satisfaction. While the relationship is not perfect, exceeding expectations corresponds with Delight, meeting expectations with Mere Satisfaction, and not meeting expectations to dissatisfaction, or the Zone of Pain (see Figure 2.5).

As we discussed, expectations are strongly influenced by experience. Therefore, if perceived quality is higher than expected, customers' subsequent expectations will generally be raised. Conversely, perceived quality that is not as good as expected will likely result in lowered expectations. Generally speaking, however, the quality level that customers believe should be provided will not decline over time. Based on these relationships we can conclude that expectations will change over time and usually increase.

The Impact of Competition

The nature and degree of competition has a direct impact on customer expectations and therefore a strong impact on the relationship between customer satisfaction and customer behavior. Two firms operating in dif-

Figure 2.4 *Expectation Hierarchy*

- Ideal
- Should
- Will (High Expectations)
- Minimally Acceptable
- Will (Low Expectations)
- Worst Possible

ferent industries may have identical satisfaction levels, yet, because of differing aggressiveness in competition, the relationship between customer satisfaction and retention in those firms may be quite different.

In particular, the more aggressive competition is in a category, the weaker will be the relationship between satisfaction and retention. Competition forces compliance to a higher performance standard, leaving fewer opportunities for any one company to distinguish itself. Likewise, consequences for noncomplying firms are harsher and more easily felt. As competition increases, the satisfaction-retention curve shifts to the right, shrinking the Zone of Delight and widening the Zone of Pain (see Figure 2.6). With this shift, it becomes easier and easier to slip from the Zone of Mere Satisfaction into the Zone of Pain. Furthermore, intense competition increases the incentives firms offer to attract and retain customers, thereby increasing customers' expectations, all of which makes it more difficult to find unique points of differentiation that will delight customers.

Figure 2.5 *Correlation Between Expectations and Satisfaction*

Adapted from: *Rust, Roland T., Anthony J. Zahorik, and Timothy L. Keiningham (1994).* Return of Quality: Measuring the Financial Impact of Your Company's Quest for Quality. *New York: McGraw-Hill Irwin. Reproduced with permission of The McGraw-Hill Companies.*

Satisfaction-Maintaining vs. Delight-Creating Attributes

Not everything that customers expect a firm to provide creates points of differentiation between competitors. In fact, many of the dimensions of a firm's offerings represent areas that customers take for granted. In highly competitive industries, strong performance on these attributes is what's considered the price of entry in the marketplace.

Good performance on attributes a customer expects seldom creates customer delight; however, poor performance creates dissatisfaction (see Figure 2.7). Because of this pattern, these attributes are called *satisfaction-maintaining attributes*. Positive performance on these attributes results only in Mere Satisfaction overall.

Other qualities have a greater positive impact on overall satisfaction when perceived performance is better. And if perceived performance is poor, the effect is not damaging to overall satisfaction (see Figure 2.8).

Figure 2.6 *Impact of Competition on Satisfaction and Delight*

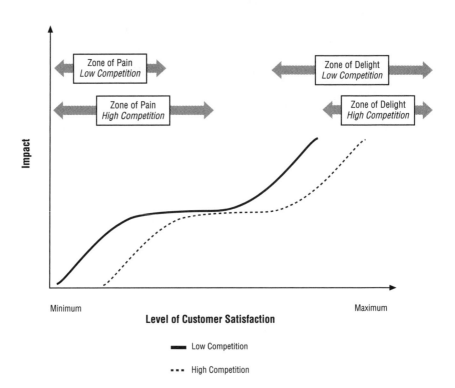

We refer to such qualities as *delight-creating attributes*. Such attributes are frequently unanticipated or unusual relative to what customers normally envision a product or service experience to entail.

Because satisfaction-maintaining attributes are core attributes, customers are likely to consider a performance in these areas to be the price of entry into the marketplace. Customers must believe that acceptable levels of performance have been achieved in these core attributes before delight-creating attributes can impact overall customer delight (see Figure 2.9).

For example, suppose that an auto dealer delivered your factory-new car to you with a broken windshield, four flat tires, chipped paint, and a blown engine. Only a member of the Addams Family would not be completely dissatisfied with the experience. Now suppose that dealer also

Figure 2.7 *Impact of Satisfaction-Maintaining Attributes on Overall Satisfaction*

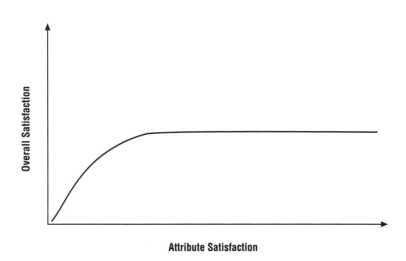

added five hundred gallons of gasoline free. This positive surprise, which might ordinarily produce delight, would not work because a basic level of satisfaction was not achieved on core components of the experience.

Summary

It is customer perceptions of quality that really count to managers. Therefore, for managers to understand how customers perceive the quality they offer, they must measure customer satisfaction. To do this effectively they must have an understanding of the psychology of customer satisfaction. In particular, they must understand what drives satisfaction (that is, prevents pain) and what drives delight.

A key step in this process is to first identify the relationships between the performance of the various attributes and customer satisfaction and delight. Some attributes will be core, or satisfaction-maintaining, while others will be delight-creating. As a result, different approaches will need to be applied based on the nature of the relationships between attributes and overall satisfaction and delight.

Figure 2.8 *Impact of Delight-Creating Attributes on Overall Satisfaction*

Implementing these new approaches requires a fundamental shift in how managers currently measure and manage customer delight. As we will see in the next chapter, current practice often ignores some basic truths and places the resulting conclusions on some very shaky foundations.

Chapter Key Notes

- Satisfaction-maintaining attributes are those attributes of a product or service that are expected and can only cause a problem when they are performed in a substandard way or are missing altogether. We must maintain these attributes at their current levels, or at a level no less as good as the competition's.
- Delight-creating attributes are attributes of a product or service that are not expected and may not be in common service. Experiencing them creates delight in the customer. We must strive to discover or create such attributes and offer them when economically feasible to high-value, targeted customers.

Figure 2.9 *The Interrelationship of Satisfaction-Maintaining and Delight-Creating Attributes on Overall Customer Satisfaction*

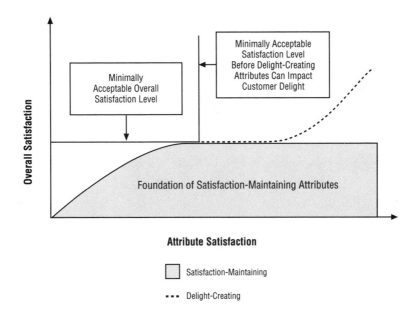

Shaky Foundations

This chapter benefited from the review and contributions of Kenneth Peterson of Marketing Metrics on a series of drafts as this chapter took shape. The authors gratefully acknowledge his assistance.

A CLASSIC PARABLE tells of two builders—one who built his house on a stone foundation, the other on sand. When a storm came, the wind and rain beat upon both houses. The house with the stone foundation was left intact. The house with the sand foundation collapsed. We all know the meaning of this often-told story. No matter how great the structure we build, for it to survive the challenges of the environment, the foundation must be solid.

Unfortunately, the foundation of many customer satisfaction measurement systems is shaky at best. As a result, efforts to delight (or even satisfy) customers have been hit or miss. And all too often managers have had to face the grim reality that their satisfaction measures show no relationship to business results. This chapter discusses some of the most common structural flaws in the current measurement and management of customer satisfaction and some solutions.

Smile Surveys

Most major companies understand the logic of satisfying their customers and fund efforts to monitor their success in doing so. So it is by no means unusual that in the late 1980s a major computer manufacturer was spending considerable amounts of money on conducting a customer satisfaction survey. This company led the PC market, and the survey was an integral part of the marketing program surrounding the company's efforts to dominate the industry. The study was conducted not only within the United States but also internationally. And, while the questionnaires did little to assure customers that they or their companies were individually known or appreciated, the inventory of questions, nevertheless, appeared to tap a wide range of issues.

From 1987 to 1994 the survey was conducted monthly among substantial samples and reported quarterly. The reports broke down scores by the company's various sales regions and by service centers. It was truly an ambitious undertaking and was likely costing $2 million or more to conduct and report in the United States alone.

Performance was evaluated on a 100-point scale. The quarterly reports were circulated throughout the company's headquarters and were the subject of regular planning meetings. On the surface it appeared that this was a sound process for maximizing customer satisfaction. But magnitude and cost are not good indicators of whether a process is built on sand or rock. Early in the survey's existence, scores were in the low eighties nationally. From 1989 through 1992 the scores showed a steady increase, rising into the low nineties (see Figure 3.1).

In contrast to the picture painted by the survey scores, the manufacturer's sales figures told an entirely different story. Throughout the duration of this seemingly thorough survey, the company's market share steadily decreased. Now, it is certainly correct that in those formative years of the PC industry the company found itself besieged by an ever-increasing range of aggressive competitors. Yet, despite the company's tenure with customers, each new competitor seemed to have little trouble finding a distinct niche with which to attract customers. One competitor entered the market by providing more suitably equipped products. Another found an easy entry by offering better customer service. Still another promised customers its PCs were a more reliable product. The obvious question is, Why didn't the company's customer satisfaction survey help it maintain a good proportion of its customer base?

Figure 3.1 *Trends in Satisfaction Ratings*

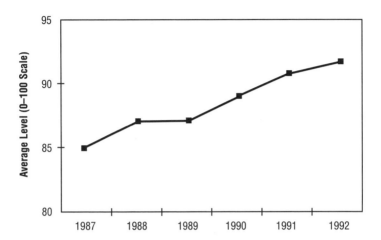

The answer can be found by analyzing the composition of the contents of the survey and the questions that were asked. Many satisfaction projects set out to measure how well a company is doing that which it believes it should do. The contents of such surveys are typically dictated by operational areas that want to prove they're doing their job well, and so they tend to measure efficiency. The customer's needs are subsumed within what the company can reasonably offer.

The old Telephone Service Attitude Measurement (TELSAM) surveys of the predivestiture AT&T operating companies are the best example of this type of survey. In these surveys customer satisfaction was measured by performance on a number of engineering-derived attributes. If the customer always got a dial tone upon lifting the receiver, if the line was never dead, then the customer was defined as being satisfied. The more particular needs that customers might have had, which might have given AT&T the opportunity to delight them, were never probed, were never measured, and were therefore never addressed.

AT&T's customers were described as satisfied based on their experiencing a number of conditions defined as "satisfiers" by engineering. Therefore, the results of the survey had little to do with the actual satisfaction of the customer. This form of evaluation always leads to serious self-delusion. As one AT&T customer-service assistant noted proudly on her resume: "Participated in special project called TELSAM. Increased customer satisfaction from 68 percent to 100 percent in a time frame of four months!"

We call surveys that measure what the company thinks it ought to be doing "smile surveys." Such surveys are essentially looking for confirmation. They don't want bad news, and they don't want to be confused by unanswered wants or new information. They are a closed-loop process: "Tell us how we're doing on *these* issues." Period.

With this background, the reality of Figure 3.2 comes as no surprise. While scores on the PC manufacturer's smile survey continued to increase (the company was simply becoming more efficient), the company's market share was heading in the opposite direction. In fact, recently this company pulled out of the PC business almost altogether!

Smile surveys are all around us. Either the survey is in its entirety prescribed by operational areas hungry for information on how well they are doing what they think they should be doing, or the questions are in part dictated internally with little or no input from customers. To avoid such myopia, one of the first reality checks must be to allow groups of customers to critique the questions of the survey. We call this process Customer Listening Groups, because that's essentially what is done—customers are listened to! Take your current satisfaction survey into a group of your customers. Ask them about the questions you're asking. Get their opinions as to what you should be asking that you're

Figure 3.2 *Trends in Satisfaction Ratings and Market Share*

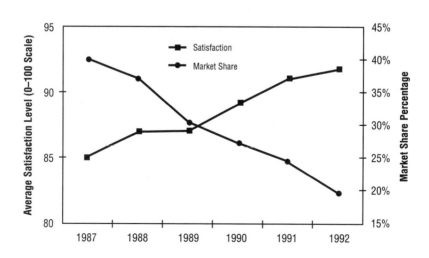

Table 3.1 *Characteristics of a Smile Survey*

Questions entirely dictated by internal departments or individuals. No customer input or review sought.

No opportunity given to customers to add issues or items—no "open-end" questions.

Questions organized around aspects of the product or service. No accommodation for the customer's experience with the product, service, or customer benefits.

Orientation to the company—"Tell Us How We're Doing."

not. Ask them how relevant the questions you're asking are to them personally. Find out what they think you want to hear from the survey. If they tell you that you want to hear how well you're doing, then throw the survey out and start over.

There are a number of indications of the type of survey you may be conducting. Table 3.1 lists the conditions that generally surround a smile survey. If your survey has one or more of these characteristics, then you should probably rethink your current survey process.

Lies, Damn Lies, and Statistics

Managers like to measure things because measurements produce numbers, and numbers are the lifeblood of companies. Complex business dynamics are reduced to ratios, indicators, and forecasts to attest financial strength and operating performance. The market valuation of an entire firm is contingent upon such numbers. The conventional reasoning is simple: "Numbers don't lie!" They provide a seemingly rational and scientific means of analyzing performance. Winners can be objectively separated from losers.

Customer satisfaction research produces lots of numbers. And measuring satisfaction is essential to managing and improving customer delight. But the numbers generated from customer satisfaction data are not like the standard financial or operating measures that managers are accustomed to handling.

Too often our need to know where we stand causes us to do silly things with satisfaction data. For example, working with a client resulted in a very unusual inquiry into the way a firm was measuring its performance relative to its competition. The inquiry read:

I can't tell how you calculated the mean in the Quality Profile, but I think there is an interesting little twist that occurs depending on how you do it. This is a synopsis of a note I put together awhile back after reading Bradley Gale's book *Managing Customer Value*. I am hesitant to say that he is doing something wrong, but I think he is. Maybe you could find time to look at this. ... Gale explains his method for calculating a "market perceived quality ratio" using data from Perdue Chicken. His table looks like this:

Table 3.2 *Example of Data Used to Calculate a Market Perceived Quality Ratio*

Attributes	Weight	Perdue	Average Competitor	Ratio	Weight times Ratio
1	2	3	4	5 = ¾	6 = 2 × 5
Yellow	10	8.1	7.2	1.13	11.3
Meat/Bone	20	9.0	7.3	1.23	24.7
Pin-feathers	20	9.2	6.5	1.42	28.3
Fresh	15	8.0	8.0	1.00	15.0
Availability	10	8.0	8.0	1.00	10.0
Brand	25	9.4	6.4	1.47	36.7
					125.9

This [Table 3.2] shows ratings for Perdue and for its competitors, and weights for the attributes customers use to judge quality. The procedure is to calculate the ratio of the ratings and multiply them by the weights and total these to get the market perceived quality ratio—125.9. ... He then suggests dividing this number by 100 to get 1.26 and states that this shows a market perceived quality rating 26 percent higher than the competition. He uses this method throughout the book.

My problem is this. When I started playing around with this, I ran into some anomalies. On the next page is a table [Table 3.3] that shows what I found. I created scores that should be equal (at least I think they should be equal). Notice that the scores in my table are balanced so that when Perdue gets a score of 3 and the competition gets a 1 for an attribute with weight 10 (Yellow meat), his competitors get a score of 3 and he gets a 1 for the other attribute with weight of 10 (Availability), and so on. Shouldn't these guys be equal? But look at the MPQR (market perceived quality ratio). Perdue is 77 percent higher than the competition.

However, if I simply exchange the columns for Competitor and Perdue [Table 3.4], the competitor now becomes 77 percent higher than Perdue, all with the same data!

Table 3.3 *New, Balanced Data for Calculating a Market Perceived Quality Ratio*

Attributes	Weight	Perdue	Average Competitor	Ratio	Weight times Ratio
1	2	3	4	$5 = \frac{3}{4}$	$6 = 2 \times 5$
Yellow	10	3.0	1.0	3.00	30.0
Meat/Bone	20	5.0	1.0	5.00	100.0
Pin-feathers	20	1.0	5.0	0.20	4.0
Fresh	15	8.0	8.0	1.00	15.0
Availability	10	1.0	3.0	0.33	3.3
Brand	25	5.0	5.0	1.00	25.0
					177.3

Table 3.4 *New, Balanced Data with Competitor and Perdue Columns Switched*

Attributes	Weight	Average Competitor	Perdue	Ratio	Weight times Ratio
1	2	3	4	$5 = \frac{3}{4}$	$6 = 2 \times 5$
Yellow	10	1.0	3.0	0.33	3.3
Meat/Bone	20	1.0	5.0	0.20	4.0
Pin-feathers	20	5.0	1.0	5.00	100.0
Fresh	15	8.0	8.0	1.00	15.0
Availability	10	3.0	1.0	3.00	30.0
Brand	25	5.0	5.0	1.00	25.0
					177.3

Am I totally missing something here? Gale is clearly good with numbers. He's an economist by training, so I need a sanity check.

A novice did not make this observation. In fact, the individual who made this inquiry was charged with assisting in the implementation of this methodology throughout the firm. Its use was widespread. Bonuses were determined based on the outcomes. And the firm was frequently cited as a best-case example of how this procedure can be used to improve market share and profits. Unfortunately, there is clearly a flaw in the methodology. Simply shifting the location of columns for the firm and its competitors dramatically impacts the interpretation of the results.

The message seems to be, caveat user, let the user beware! Even when a well-discussed technique is utilized, a manager still needs to be prudent in his or her reliance on the results.

Can't Get Real

Managers are accustomed to dealing with "real" numbers. Standard business numbers such as revenues, expenses, inventory levels, and scrap rates all follow the basic rules of arithmetic. The numbers are both *ordinal* (designate rank order), and *interval* (each successive integer is exactly the same interval higher than the preceding one), and they conform to ratio qualities (a profit of $500 million is twice a profit of $250 million).

Ratings on a satisfaction scale, however, are not real numbers in the mathematical sense. Satisfaction ratings are certainly ordinal, but they lack both interval and ratio qualities. A company has no idea how survey respondents use the scale. It can be certain, however, that the behavioral

Figure 3.3 Impact of Satisfaction and Delight

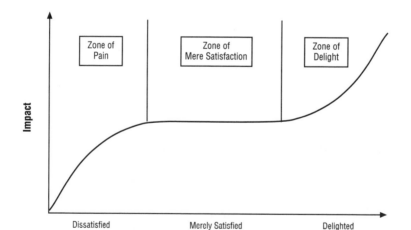

Adapted from: Rust, Roland T., Anthony J. Zahorik, and Timothy L. Keiningham (1994). Return of Quality: Measuring the Financial Impact of Your Company's Quest for Quality. *New York: McGraw-Hill Irwin. Reproduced with permission of The McGraw-Hill Companies.*

consequences of different rating levels in the satisfaction scale will almost never be linear (see Figure 3.3). Based on customer behavior, customers appear to view some levels of satisfaction more closely than others when rating their level of satisfaction.

Adding to the difficulty, satisfaction scales do not have an absolute zero point. Assigning a zero is completely arbitrary, similar to the zero point on a Fahrenheit thermometer. This makes comparisons difficult. For example, it is not possible to say that one rating level is twice that of another level. That's equivalent to the meteorologist saying sixty-four degrees Fahrenheit is twice as hot as thirty-two degrees. On a Celsius scale, the weather forecaster would have to say it was infinitely hotter, as thirty-two degrees Fahrenheit equals zero degrees Celsius. As you can see, neither statement would be correct.

While all of this may seem self-evident and elementary, even the most respected firms routinely ignore it. Managers commonly state that their firm's customer satisfaction/quality ratings are some percentage better (or worse) than competition. Researchers routinely convert satisfaction scales from prior research to match a current scale for historical comparison purposes (for example, a 5-point scale used in prior research is arithmetically converted to a currently used 10-point scale). The most common mistake, however, is the misuse of mean (average) satisfaction scores.

Does This Mean Mean What I Think It Means?

A common brainteaser reads:

> You are taking a two-mile trip and want to average sixty miles per hour. After finishing the first mile, you averaged thirty miles per hour. How fast would you have to travel the second mile to average sixty miles per hour for the entire trip?

If you answered ninety miles per hour, so that the arithmetic mean would be sixty miles per hour, think again. The fact is, you couldn't complete your journey averaging sixty miles per hour no matter how fast you went the second mile. To average sixty miles per hour requires traveling an average speed of one mile per minute. Likewise, traveling thirty miles per hour requires traveling an average speed of one mile every two minutes. Given that you are only traveling two miles, averaging sixty miles per hour requires reaching your destination in two minutes. Those two minutes, however, were used up traveling the first mile.

So what does this brainteaser have to do with measuring customer delight? Just as this example demonstrates, our natural tendency is to rely on simple averages to solve otherwise complex problems. Sometimes that inclination leads to wrong answers.

Score averages are the most widespread method of communicating customer satisfaction results. Arithmetic means conveniently condense information, are easy to compute, are conceptually simple, and can easily be compared to other means when using similar satisfaction scales. Unfortunately, all of these positive attributes, combined with the desire to simplify numerical information, cause even people with Ph.D.s to lose perspective of the problem they are addressing and misuse the mean as a summation of a situation. A host of problems arises when one relies too heavily on mean averages to address customer satisfaction data. Here are just a few:

• *Problem 1: The mean is perceived as the typical value.* When summarizing customer satisfaction data the mean almost never represents the typical value. Imagine that only two customers were surveyed. One customer's satisfaction level is categorized as a 5, while the other is categorized as a 3. The average is a 4, but that can hardly be called typical since neither customer selected 4. Furthermore, for samples of any size, mean scores are seldom whole numbers. Rather, they fall between explicit categories (for example, 3.4, 2.9, and so on), which makes interpretation even more ambiguous.

More and more we believe it is appropriate to consider keeping data disaggregated. Consider tracking how many customers' scores increase from one measurement period to another and compare that with those customers whose scores decrease. This offers a method to measure the overall status of the customer base while keeping a fix on each individual's scores.

• *Problem 2: Mean scores are believed to take on interval-scale properties.* As noted earlier, satisfaction scales are ordinal but not interval. In many cases the numbers assigned to the satisfaction level are completely arbitrary. Take, for example, a scale that asks customers to select from the following satisfaction levels: Very Satisfied, Somewhat Satisfied, Neither Satisfied Nor Dissatisfied, Somewhat Dissatisfied, and Very Dissatisfied. The exact numerical values to be assigned to the categories is completely determined by the researcher and is done in an arbitrary, though not entirely illogical, manner.

Typically, such scales are assigned consecutive integers (such as 1 to 5 or −2 to +2), and virtually always the numbers assigned are equal intervals apart. (For discussion purposes, we will refer to such rating systems as "traditional.") We know, however, that behavioral consequences related to the different rating levels will almost never be linear. This fact poses problems when interpreting changes in average satisfaction levels.

Suppose customers are asked to rate their level of satisfaction on a traditional 10-point scale, with a 1 being Completely Dissatisfied and a 10 being Completely Satisfied. Now suppose that the corresponding impact on customers' repurchase behavior for this 10-point scale follows the S-shaped curve in Figure 3.4a. Let's assume that the impact axis for this curve corresponds to the "true" scale. Based on that assumption, the interval between scale points varies considerably (see Figure 3.4b).

To see how this incongruity can create problems, assume that each satisfaction level on the 10-point scale was selected by 10 percent of a firm's customers (see Table 3.5). The mean score would be 5.5. Using the same assumptions for the hypothetical true scale, however, the mean is 4.6. In this case, the traditional scale gives the impression that mean satisfaction levels are much higher than the true scale shows them to be.

Furthermore, the traditional scale will overstate the impact of shifts in satisfaction for rating levels 2 through 6. According to the true scale,

Figure 3.4a *Sample Relationship Between Satisfaction Levels and Impact on Customer Behavior*

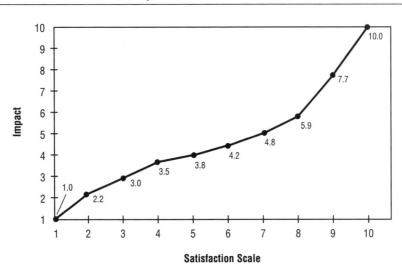

Figure 3.4b *Sample Relationship Between Traditional and Hypothetical True Scales*

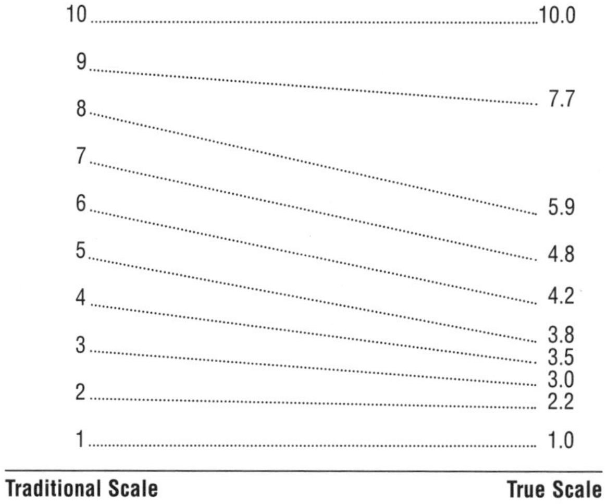

Traditional Scale	True Scale
10	10.0
9	
8	7.7
7	
6	5.9
5	4.8
4	4.2
3	3.8
	3.5
	3.0
2	2.2
1	1.0

these satisfaction levels are viewed as being relatively close to one another, all having intervals less than 1. Likewise, the traditional scale will understate the impact of shifts from 7 through 10, as according to the true scale these satisfaction levels are relatively far apart, all having intervals greater than 1.

On a practical level, improving mean satisfaction levels will prove more difficult at some points in the scale than at others. In the case of the hypothetical true scale used in Figure 3.4b, improving mean scores will be much easier at the lower half of the scale than at the upper half. In addition, it gets progressively harder to move satisfaction levels for each increment above 7 on the traditional scale because the size of the interval (as shown on the true scale) increases at every successive increment above 7.

• *Problem 3: Mean scores are thought to represent good action targets.* Managers are accustomed to being judged based on achieving thresholds, whether they be earnings, inventory turns, or defect rates. Proof of success is contingent upon meeting the numbers. And in all fairness, setting objectives demonstrates importance and demands accountability.

The problem in customer delight management, however, is that goals are frequently based on achieving mean satisfaction levels without an understanding of the underlying dynamics of satisfaction data. As a result,

Table 3.5 *Example of Difference in Mean Scores Between Traditional and Hypothetical True Scale*

	Traditional Scale			True Scale		
Scale Rating	Percent of Customers			Scale Rating	Percent of Customers	
(1)	(2)	(1 × 2)		(3)	(4)	(3 × 4)
1	10.0%	0.10		1.0	10.0%	0.10
2	10.0%	0.20		2.2	10.0%	0.22
3	10.0%	0.30		3.0	10.0%	0.30
4	10.0%	0.40		3.5	10.0%	0.35
5	10.0%	0.50		3.8	10.0%	0.38
6	10.0%	0.60		4.2	10.0%	0.42
7	10.0%	0.70		4.8	10.0%	0.48
8	10.0%	0.80		5.9	10.0%	0.59
9	10.0%	0.90		7.7	10.0%	0.77
10	10.0%	1.00		10.0	10.0%	1.00
	Mean	5.50			Mean	4.61

mean, or average, satisfaction levels frequently do not represent a good measure of success.

For example, suppose managers were assigned target satisfaction objectives of 7.5 on a 10-point traditional scale. An easy way to imagine achieving this objective is for 50 percent of customers to rate their satisfaction level a 7 and the remaining 50 percent to rate their satisfaction level an 8. Likewise, one could achieve a 7.5 by having customers evenly divided into levels 6, 7, 8, and 9. Unfortunately, both scenarios are not equal in terms of impact on the firm. Table 3.6 shows how mean scores, using the true scale introduced earlier, would change for various customer distributions that are equivalent to a 7.5 mean on the traditional scale. In this case, as more customers reach higher satisfaction levels, mean scores for the true scale increase, suggesting that the impact to the firm is greater. Now consider the pragmatic impact of a management team setting improvement goals without truly understanding the underlying asymmetry of response. An improvement of one point might be somewhat easily achieved at a midscale satisfaction of 5 or 6. But what if management requires a 1-point increase from a base of 8? The required effort will be considerably greater, the burden on the workforce much more difficult.

Even without knowing the true scale, the first scenario in which no customer rated his or her satisfaction level higher than an 8 is intuitively less desirable than the second, where 25 percent of customers rate their satisfaction higher than an 8. At lower levels of satisfaction, rarely is there competitive differentiation in terms of perceived service quality. Therefore, under the first scenario it is possible, even realistic, to imagine that 100 percent of customers believe that the firm is the same or worse than the competition. With the second scenario, in which 25 percent of customers are closer to the upper extreme, this is much less likely. The mean, however, does not distinguish one scenario from the other.

It is for these reasons that we believe the "top-box score" (percent rating service as "delightful" or "beyond expectation") is a better tool for planning and tracking customer delight.

Table 3.6 *Example of Difference in Mean Scores Based on Distribution of Customer Satisfaction Levels Between Traditional and Hypothetical True Scale*

Traditional Scale				True Scale		
Scale Rating	Percent of Customers			Scale Rating	Percent of Customers	
(1)	(2)	(1 × 2)		(3)	(4)	(3 × 4)
7	50.0%	3.5		4.8	50.0%	2.4
8	50.0%	4.0		5.9	50.0%	3.0
	Mean 7.5				Mean 5.4	
6	25.0%	1.5		4.2	25.0%	1.1
7	25.0%	1.8		4.8	25.0%	1.2
8	25.0%	2.0		5.9	25.0%	1.5
9	25.0%	2.3		7.7	25.0%	1.9
	Mean 7.5				Mean 5.7	
5	16.7%	0.8		3.8	16.7%	0.6
6	16.7%	1.0		4.2	16.7%	0.7
7	16.7%	1.2		4.8	16.7%	0.8
8	16.7%	1.3		5.9	16.7%	1.0
9	16.7%	1.5		7.7	16.7%	1.3
10	16.7%	1.7		10.0	16.7%	1.7
	Mean 7.5				Mean 6.1	

Summary of Points 1, 2, and 3

- Numeric values assigned to customer satisfaction ratings are largely misapplied, misused, and misunderstood.

- The assumed, though incorrect, linearity and interval properties of satisfaction ratings can cause both inequities and inconsistencies in management and in assigning rewards (to both performance and remedial efforts).

- Numeric averages, or means, are not a reliable way to summarize or track periodic performance.

What Is Significant?

Statistical significance is designed to avoid accepting something as true when in reality it is false (called a Type 1 error—think "accepting a falsehood"). It is similar to the directions given to juries in criminal court proceedings that a finding of guilt requires that evidence be presented that proves the defendant culpable beyond a reasonable doubt. But just as this high standard in the court increases the probability that a truly guilty person will be set free, high statistical significance levels increase the probability that we will reject a true difference (called a Type 2 error—think "rejecting a truth").

Statistical significance levels indicate how likely something is to occur by chance. As was mentioned, the most common level used to determine if something is good enough to be believed is the 95 percent level of significance, or more precisely the "level of statistical confidence." This means that there is a 5 percent chance of accepting something as true based on the sample data when in fact in the population it is false.

A significance level of 80 percent means that there is a 20 percent chance of accepting something as true when in fact it is false. This allowance is 15 percentage points larger than the commonly used 95 percent significance level. But at the 80 percent level, if we simply accepted the difference as real, we would still be right four out of five times. In life, how often are we right 80 percent of the time? Ignoring such differences (identified at lower levels of precision) results in significant opportunity loss. We literally lose the opportunity to identify and act on real influencers of customer delight.

The high opportunity costs caused by an inflexible overreliance on significance levels to justify decisions has caused some to question the focus of significance testing. It has been proposed that, instead of a significance test, for the purpose of management decision making we should consider a statistical *in*significance test. This changes the focus of the basic question we ask when we use significance tests. The traditional question is, "How do I minimize accepting a wrong answer?" Now the question becomes, "How do I minimize rejecting a right answer?"

Are odds of 1 out of 4 that the results occurred by chance too high? Do we want to dismiss odds of 1 out of 3 out of hand? We are not advocating rejecting significance testing, nor do we expect managers to accept differences based on near 50-50 probabilities. Significance criteria, however, must be based on the nature of the decision to be made and the risk to the company of implementing the decision. Therefore, decision rules should be adjusted so that the ratio of Type 1 to Type 2 errors is consistent with the costs and benefits of both types of errors.

A decision that will represent a significant capital investment would necessarily require a higher significance threshold than would lower risk items. The key to making these assessments, however, must be based on practical managerial implications and not simply arbitrary statistical thresholds. To say that the likelihood against a chance occurrence is significant at the 95 percent level and not at the 93 percent level doesn't make much sense. Unfortunately, virtually all managers make decisions as if it did.

Is This Significant?

In a lecture at Vanderbilt University, Roger Sawquist, former CEO of Calgene, Inc., maker of the first genetically altered food for consumer use, the Flavr Savr tomato, explained why he never wanted his company's scientists to speak to the public. To paraphrase his explanation, scientists never say that something will not happen, even if it has an infinitesimally small probability of occurring. Being scientists, virtually *nothing* is considered impossible, no matter how improbable. Sawquist, on the other hand, noted that when the probability is minuscule, he personally had no problem stating that such an occurrence "absolutely would never occur!"

So what do Flavr Savr tomatoes have to do with measuring customer delight? Measuring customer satisfaction results in an abundance of data. Managers ultimately want to use the data to guide their decisions and to separate winners from losers. Invariably, at some point managers are going to inquire about the significance of the numbers.

But as the statements by Sawquist illustrate, the criteria for what is considered significant can be truly arbitrary. While the Food and Drug Administration (FDA) considered the safety of the Flavr Savr tomato to be well documented, granting its approval for Calgene to market the product in 1994, Flavr Savr tomatoes did not catch on in part because of the fears some groups of consumers had of genetically modified food. Statistically, the risk of genetically engineered vegetables causing humans any adverse effect was determined to be less than 1 in 100 million. Yet, the statistical significance level of risk did not absolutely rule out the possibility of danger; it simply assigned it an incredibly low likelihood. Opposing consumer groups viewed the significance level differently; they were unwilling to accept any likelihood of ill effects, no matter how small.

Testing for statistical significance has become standard operating procedure for most researchers. The preceding example highlights the somewhat arbitrary nature of a supposedly objective and scientific criterion. When examining data, the hardest part of a manager's job may well be assessing the information and setting the appropriate criteria to determine its "managerial" importance.

Unfortunately, managers often misuse the concept of significance. In everyday English, *significant* means "important," while in statistics it means "probably true" (that is, not a random occurrence). The difficulty is that a finding may be true without it being important!

Another mistake managers frequently make is associating statistical significance with "bigness" of a result. They often think that the difference between two levels must be large and therefore worthy of consideration in the analysis. That, however, is also not necessarily the case. Statistical significance between two means actually depends upon four factors:

1. Absolute difference in size

2. Variance of responses around the mean

3. Size of the sample

4. Level of precision at which the difference is being considered

In other words, at some sample size, virtually all differences will be determined statistically significant. For example, a large automotive client had sample sizes so large that differences as small as .002 could be determined to be statistically significant! While such small differences may be true, clearly they are not managerially relevant. The issue of "false precision" abounds throughout satisfaction research. It's best to keep in mind an observation by Scott Adams, creator of Dilbert: "The creator of the universe works in mysterious ways. But he uses a base ten counting system and likes round numbers." While Adams was obviously joking, he is talking about a basic truth: With regard to customer satisfaction data, assigning values to the hundredth decimal place may be mathematically precise, but it is not very informative.

It matters little if the results from your analysis of the satisfaction data are statistically significant if they do not correspond to changes in customer behavior. As noted earlier, the relationship between satisfaction and customer behavior is almost never linear, and as a result, improvement efforts that produce small changes in satisfaction levels tend to be unprofitable. Therefore, operationally defining trivial effects before starting a customer satisfaction program, based on both previous research or theory, allows thinking in terms of substantive versus nonsubstantive differences, as opposed to significant versus nonsignificant.

The Problem with Numbers

Many companies have adopted a "balanced scorecard" measurement system to incorporate an external perspective into their traditional measures of business performance. Part of this measurement system is a focus on customer service and satisfaction. In fact, the balanced scorecard has been singularly successful in helping customer satisfaction achieve a new status within many North American corporations.

The system is a response to the belief that many corporate boards and CEOs have been fixating solely on financial numbers as indicators of success and have thus oriented companies to short-term fixes. The balanced scorecard incorporates nonfinancial measures of corporate performance with financial measures. Along with the traditional financial and internal efficiency criteria, which tend to be short-term in focus, it includes learning/growth and customer orientation, indicators of longer-term per-

Summarizing Significance

- Statistical significance levels show how likely a result is to have occurred by chance.

- Statistical significance between two means actually depends upon four factors: the absolute difference in size, the variance of responses around the mean, the size of the sample, and the level of precision at which the difference is being considered. Therefore, at some sample size, virtually all differences will be determined statistically significant.

- Statistical significance does not equate to importance. In statistics *significant* means "probably true." A finding may be true, however, without it being important.

formance, as missing, valuable criteria. By using these additional criteria, balanced scorecard advocates argue, corporate management will bring more balance to the measures it uses to score its performance.

The customer-orientation dimension of this management view ought to be assessed through five measures:

1. Market share

2. Customer acquisition

3. Customer retention

4. Customer satisfaction

5. Customer profitability

Most companies gather data about their market share through third-party industry monitors, or "clearing houses." Such estimates are based on industrywide sales, shipments, or customer registrations. But when it comes to customer acquisition and retention, information starts to get very vague; most companies haven't even begun to understand customer profitability. Customer satisfaction is the one measure besides market share that a company can most easily acquire. It will come as little surprise then that the customer-orientation cell of the balanced scorecard is often almost solely defined by customer satisfaction. Thus the balanced scorecard has gained overnight the visibility and acceptance for customer satisfaction that strategic quality leaders have long been advocating.

Unfortunately, this new-found visibility and acceptance bring disadvantages as well. The balanced scorecard accords customer satisfaction, a main measure for the customer-orientation criterion, a place as one of four numbers, one of four information blocks in what many today are calling the corporate "instrument panel." But just as one superficially looks to one's automobile instrument panel to determine how fast one is traveling in raw numbers, so too does the balanced scorecard focus upper management's attention on a *number*, the *score*, rather than on the *concept* of customer satisfaction. The attention and focus on the number promulgates a companywide focus on numbers—not causes, not solutions, but numbers. The battle cry becomes, "Let's get the *number* up!" Instead the reaction should be, "Let's find out why not enough of our customers are delighted!" The warning should result in a review of how to better satisfy customers, but the stampede is on to simply raise the number.

And numbers can be improved in many different ways. All too frequently in corporations using a balanced scorecard the improvement process includes one or more of the following actions:

- Redefining the rating-scale positions that count toward customer satisfaction (for example, top two boxes as opposed to top box)
- Changing the weights of rating-scale labels (changing points assigned to "excellent" from 60 to 45 to give a higher number to "very good," 35 up from 25)
- Reexamining who is being asked the questions in an effort to heighten scores ("We're obviously not interviewing the right customers. Let's ask the sales department to identify those customers we should be interviewing.")

- Excluding so-called outlier scores—generally those scores that are below a minimum threshold (Scores of "poor" are obviously very bitter people or customers with severe problems; therefore, they are uncharacteristic of the customer base in general.)
- Rewording the rating scales, making top-box ratings easier for customers to apply to their experiences (for example, changing the rating label "excellent" to "very good")
- Contacting customers prior to conducting the survey, informing them of the importance of the survey and sometimes even asking them for high ratings

It's easy to see that when attention is focused on numbers, it's always tempting to *fix the score*, rather than to *fix the store*. And so often the score is what gets fixed. This satisfies management with a higher number but leaves customers in exactly the same condition they were in prior to the initiation of the measurement process.

Summary

There are many ways that managers delude themselves with customer satisfaction information. The sad truth is that the vast majority of satisfaction measurement programs contain one or more of the problems detailed in this chapter, and the results are frequently disastrous. But the blame might never be correctly assigned to a poor underlying model or to a naive interpretation of the information. Instead, operational personnel may be faulted for their failure to promote change and managers pressured to produce unreasonable results.

Our discussion of the "traditional" continuum of satisfaction versus the "true" continuum hopefully will give readers the incentive to consider more fully how numerical values are being assigned to scale positions and how they are being extrapolated for managerial directives. The false certainty that numerical values convey and lack of knowledge of the limitations of most numerical scores are responsible for many interpretational problems.

In order to succeed, we must become better mechanics and interpret numerical scores with more statistical discipline. Consistently achieving customer delight demands a clear understanding of what satisfies and what delights customers. Without that foundation, no structure we build to improve customer delight is built to last.

Chapter Key Notes

- Statistical analysis in customer satisfaction research is as problematic as in any other endeavor. Unfortunately, too often customer satisfaction managers rely on their partner-suppliers or their own statistical consultants to summarize results. These individuals are frequently summarizing or interpreting results incorrectly because they fail to honor the limitations of satisfaction data. In other cases, they are making unfounded assumptions about the linearity of results.
- Be wary of summary statistics like means (statistical averages). While means offer a convenient measure by which to summarize data, they eliminate the option to view the actual distribution of data from customers.
- Maintaining data at the individual customer level is a more definitive way of tracking actual improvements or regressions in satisfaction. It can be more compelling to management to hear that 12 percent of a firm's customer satisfaction scores increased from the previous period, as opposed to reporting an increase of 0.3 points (from 3.8 to 4.1 on a 5-point scale) in the average satisfaction rating.

Cracking the Code

This chapter was written by Eugene W. Anderson and Vikas Mittal in conjunction with the authors. Parts of this chapter were included in "Strengthening the Satisfaction-Profit Chain" by Anderson and Mittal, which appeared in the November 2000 issue of the Journal of Service Research.

Eugene W. Anderson is associate professor of marketing at the University of Michigan Business School. He holds a Ph.D. in marketing and statistics from the University of Chicago Graduate School of Business, as well as a B.Sc. and an M.B.A. from the University of Illinois at Urbana-Champaign. His research interest is in how individuals evaluate consumption experience, the behavioral consequences of such evaluations, and the economic and strategic consequences for the firm.

Vikas Mittal is assistant professor of marketing at the Katz Graduate School of Business, University of Pittsburgh. He holds a Ph.D. in business administration from Temple University and a B.B.A. from the University of Michigan. His research is in understanding issues related to satisfaction, repurchase intentions, repurchase behavior, and profitability.

TWO CENTURIES AGO, a twenty-eight-year-old Napoleon arrived in the Nile Delta with plans to seize Egypt, which was then a part of the Ottoman Empire, in order to disrupt Britain's critical overland trade route to India. The Egyptians were no match for the experienced French troops. But Napoleon's dreams of further conquest were shattered almost immediately after his victory when ten days later Admiral Horatio Nelson utterly destroyed the French fleet. Napoleon's imperialistic adventurism and ultimate defeat, however, resulted in one of the single most important discoveries in the history of archaeology. On July 15, 1799, French soldiers preparing the foundations for an extension to Fort Julien, at Rosetta (or Rashid, as it is known in Arabic) in northern Egypt, uncovered a large, polished, tombstone-shaped slab of black basalt incised with writing in three different scripts: hieroglyphics, an Egyptian script called "demotic," and Greek.

The officer in charge immediately recognized its significance. Because the final paragraph in Greek stated that all three texts contained identical messages, it was evident that this represented the beginning of one of history's great intellectual adventures. A key had been found for translating the heretofore-indecipherable hieroglyphics, the formal and ceremonial language of the pharaohs that covered most of Egypt's monuments and artifacts. Twenty years later (the time required to crack the code) Jean-Francois Champollion published his decipherment. With this publication, the mysteries of ancient Egypt were unlocked. To quote *Life* magazine, "This breakthrough, and the translations it produced, led to revelations both humbling and exhilarating."

Decoding Delight

For most managers, deciphering customer delight data is akin to trying to make sense of ancient Egyptian hieroglyphs. The importance of the information is widely acknowledged, but most companies lack a "satisfaction Rosetta stone." As a result, managers struggle to create improvement programs and are provided virtually no help in estimating the returns from their efforts.

Many firms have watched their performance improve on key-driver attributes only to discover that their overall delight scores have failed to show a corresponding increase. At other times, improvement in overall satisfaction scores has failed to have a demonstrable positive impact on customer retention or corporate profits.

Unfortunately, there has been no seminal discovery of a single Rosetta stone for interpreting customer satisfaction data. But thanks to the work of many different researchers, the relationship between customer delight and customer behavior is becoming clearer. In effect, we have the "code" for satisfaction tied to the "code" for behavior and can now begin to decipher the hieroglyphics of customer delight.

A Key Discovery

The Delight Progression is the central chain of effects that leads from service performance to market share and profits. This sequence of events consists of three stages, Delight, Retention, and Profit, and the links to and between them (see Figure 4.1).

The first thing to note is that customer perceptions of the performance of various service/product attributes (that is, customer satisfaction with performance) lead to ratings of satisfaction with the firm as a whole. Satisfaction through delight, in turn, impacts customers' willingness to remain as customers of the firm (retention), which ultimately impacts the firm's market share and profits. Not only are these interfaces intuitive, but they have also been confirmed through a large body of research. Despite this acknowledged linkage, there is no shortage of breakdowns between the various interfaces in the Delight Progression.

Many of these anomalies can be explained by the recent discovery of two important characteristics of the interfaces in the Delight Progression.

Figure 4.1 *The Delight Progression*

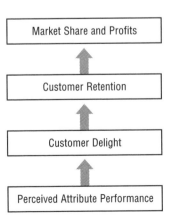

1. The interfaces are often *asymmetric.* That is, the impact of an increase is different from the impact of an equivalent decrease, not only in terms of direction but also in terms of magnitude. For the performance-satisfaction interface, this means that, for some attributes, a decrease will have a greater impact on satisfaction than an equivalent increase in the same attribute. Such cases are said to have *negative asymmetry.* With other attributes, an increase will have a greater impact on satisfaction than an equivalent decrease. In such cases, the relationship between performance and customer satisfaction exhibits *positive asymmetry.*

2. The interfaces can be *nonlinear.* At certain points in the Delight Progression, nonlinearity appears in the form of *diminishing returns.* That is, each additional one-unit increase in an input has a smaller impact than the preceding one-unit increase. For the performance-satisfaction interface, consecutive increases in performance levels (in certain types of attributes) will have less and less of an impact on satisfaction. At other points in the chain, the nonlinearity shows up in the form of *increasing returns,* in which the impact of improvement is greater with each consecutive increase.

The next section describes the asymmetric and nonlinear nature of the three interfaces.

Delight Progression Interface 1: Perceived Performance Leads to Customer Delight

Figure 4.2 illustrates three commonly found relationships between the performance of different types of product and service attributes and overall satisfaction. Part A of Figure 4.2 depicts the conventional view of the relationship between performance attributes and customer satisfaction. In fact, most customer satisfaction programs naively conceive of this surprisingly complicated relationship in this manner. The relationship is considered symmetric and linear; a one-unit change in performance is expected to lead to an equal change in overall satisfaction whether the change impacts midlevel performance scores or extremely good or bad scores.[1]

Figure 4.2 *Satisfaction-Performance Relationship*

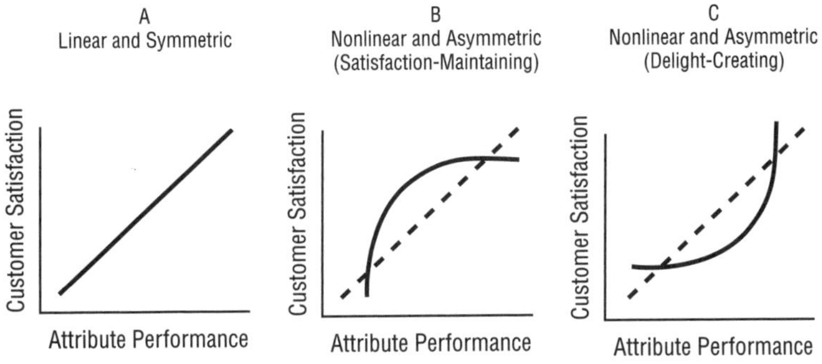

A
Linear and Symmetric

B
Nonlinear and Asymmetric
(Satisfaction-Maintaining)

C
Nonlinear and Asymmetric
(Delight-Creating)

Note: The dotted line in B and C represents a linear approximation of the nonlinear relationship shown.

Satisfaction-Maintaining Attributes

The fact is, in most instances the relationship between perceived performance and satisfaction, instead of being symmetric and linear, follows one of the patterns shown in Figure 4.2, Parts B and C. Part B depicts a negatively asymmetric and nonlinear performance attribute with diminishing returns in its impact on satisfaction. Here, changes at lower levels of perceived attribute performance have a greater impact on customer satisfaction than changes at the upper levels. Moreover, due to the inherent nonlinearity, performance changes (improvements or declines) from low-level performance will show much greater change in satisfaction than performance changes from middle or high performance levels. This is an application of the classic diminishing-returns model.

Performance attributes that exhibit this pattern are generally satisfaction-maintaining attributes—in other words, they maintain mere satisfaction. Examples of satisfaction-maintaining attributes include:

For Cellular Telephone Service

- Regularity with which a subscriber is able to place a call
- Absence of dropped calls
- Clarity of calls

For a Mutual Fund

- Fund performance

- Clear communication of fund information

Satisfaction-maintaining attributes are core attributes that customers generally take for granted. As such, they are likely to exhibit negative asymmetry and diminishing returns in their ability to increase customer satisfaction. In highly competitive industries, strong performance on these attributes is the price of survival in the marketplace; without them a brand or business is dead.

Delight-Creating Attributes

Figure 4.2c depicts attribute performance with an impact on overall satisfaction that is positively asymmetric and nonlinear with increasing returns. In this case, performance changes (improvements or declines) at higher levels of perceived attribute performance have a greater impact on satisfaction than changes at lower levels. At the same time, performance changes occurring near the upper extreme of the scale are more consequential than performance changes occurring in the middle range. Such attributes are usually delight-creating attributes and are frequently unanticipated or unusual relative to what customers envision receiving from a product or experiencing in a service. Examples of delight-creating attributes include:

For Airline Travel

- Ticket purchase and validation onboard the aircraft

- Sleeper seats

- Traveler services and amenities at destination airports

For Retailers

- Gift registries

- Free gift wrap

- Concierge or personal-shopper services

The asymmetric and nonlinear relationships depicted in Parts B and C of Figure 4.2 have been observed in a host of different industries, including health care, automotive, and banking. Why? Customers evaluate performance on the basis of relative-performance changes rather than absolute-performance changes. Consider a satisfaction-maintaining attribute, such as miles per gallon for automobiles. An increase of ten miles per gallon has less impact on overall satisfaction for a car with an already high performance level, say forty miles per gallon, than when the customer's reference point is much lower, such as twenty miles per gallon. Moreover, such an increase will probably be less consequential than a decrease of the same amount from the same midrange reference point. An increase of ten miles per gallon from a starting point of twenty-five miles per gallon is less likely to produce delight than a decrease of ten miles per gallon is to cause dissatisfaction, or pain.

Other Theories

The notion of satisfaction-maintaining and delight-creating attributes is compatible with ideas set forward by at least two other theorists. Noriaki Kano first described a system in which not all variables contributed to overall satisfaction in an equal way in several papers (in Japanese) dating back to 1984. Kano theorized that performance variables by which customers judge products and services can probably be classified into one of three types:

   1. Expected, basic performance attributes. These describe the basic functions that customers expect from a product or service. Without these attributes, a product or service is unacceptable, but their presence in no way delights customers.

   2. One-dimensional performance attributes. These attributes tend to produce linear returns to satisfaction. An example would be coverage for a cellular telephone system: the broader the coverage, the happier its customers will be.

   3. Attractor, delighter performance attributes. These are totally unexpected attributes, which, if present, generate for customers considerable delight and pleasure. They offer opportunities for differentiation that can build a loyal following for a product or service.

The Types of Performance Attributes

Not all performance attributes are equal; there are two types. They differ in satisfaction's response to changes in their perceived performance, and neither are linear nor symmetric.

Satisfaction-Maintaining Attributes

- Expected by customers

- Incapable of delighting but necessary to survive

- Manager's goal: achieve parity performance on these attributes but no more. Don't cut back for cost savings

- Generally display diminishing returns to satisfaction beyond a parity-performance level

Delight-Creating Attributes

- Surprise customers, creating delight

- Manager's goal: create these attributes and be first in one's category to introduce them

- Create a unique point of differentiation

- Usually display accelerating returns to satisfaction beyond a minimal-performance level

Kano's message is consistent with the current message: Don't heavily invest in basic attributes; payback will be scant if any at all. Basic attributes are threshold attributes. Either a product or service has them and survives or lacks them and perishes. The real competitive advantage, according to Kano's theory, is in identifying attractor performance attributes and then offering them before one's competitors do. This affords an enterprise a unique point of differentiation and attraction for current and new customers alike.

Professor Richard Oliver, in his review of satisfaction, describes a similar system of three types of performance attributes. Oliver identifies his attributes according to whether they are expected or not and the directionality of their influence:

1. Monovalent dissatisfiers. These attributes are not consciously judged, but highly conspicuous when they fail, capable of causing major dissatisfaction.

2. Bivalent satisfiers. Attributes in this category are capable of causing satisfaction or dissatisfaction in a fairly linear way.

3. Monovalent satisfiers. These are attributes that are unexpected and cause surprise when offered, creating delight.

Implications

Treating the performance-satisfaction interface as symmetric and linear leads to erroneous priorities for creating customer delight. Figure 4.3 summarizes what happens if the performance-satisfaction interface is modeled mistakenly as symmetric and linear. The impact differs by the type of attribute. For satisfaction-maintaining attributes, the linear approach overestimates the impact of changes at the extremes and underestimates the impact of changes nearer the customer's reference point, which is typically the middle of the performance measurement scale. For delight-creating attributes, the linear approach underestimates the impact of changes at extreme levels and overestimates the impact of changes in the midrange of performance.

The problem is even more pronounced by the fact that customer satisfaction is directly tied to the current level of performance of the various attributes. In other words, customers use current performance levels as their benchmarks by which to assess change. As a result, delight-creating attributes with current low performance levels may not appear important, but their impact might be great if performance were improved. Likewise, satisfaction-maintaining attributes with currently high performance levels may appear unimportant. In such cases, reallocating resources from

Figure 4.3 *How Assumptions of Linearity and Symmetry Affect Classification of Attribute Importance*

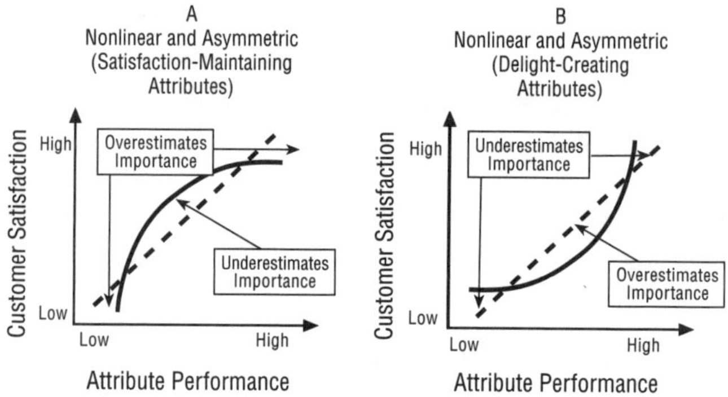

Note: The dotted line represents a linear approximation of the nonlinear relationship shown.

them to other attributes could prove disastrous, suddenly shifting performance on these attributes into regions where small decreases in perceived performance result in large losses in satisfaction.

Satisfaction programs have acknowledged the need to focus improvement efforts on a limited set of performance attributes. Management's process has generally been to identify the most important attributes (the key drivers) and then selectively increasing performance on the subset of these attributes for which current performance is average or low. The operational mechanism for accomplishing this is called a *quadrant chart* or a *performance-importance grid*.[2] Hopefully it is evident that so simplistic an approach to planning will not fairly represent the more complex relationships we believe exist.

Given the asymmetry described here, both increasing positive performance *and* mitigating negative performance should be recognized as possibly effective goals depending on the nature of the attribute (delight-creating or satisfaction-maintaining) and the current level of perceived performance.

Managerial Consequences

Contrary to current industry practice, our message is quite clear: understand the nature of your performance variables *before* establishing your improvement goals; otherwise, it is easy to misallocate attention and resources to variables that will fail to provide adequate responsiveness in terms of movement toward delight. We begin building a Customer Delight Manifesto, with three of six guiding principles:

• **Customer Delight Principle 1:** The mechanisms customers use to judge the adequacy of products, services, and their providers, the so-called performance attributes, are not homogeneous as implied by conventional measurement and interpretation. Instead, they can be classified according to their ultimate consequence: maintaining satisfaction or creating delight.

• **Customer Delight Principle 2:** For satisfaction-maintaining attributes, first insure against negative performance rather than improving positive performance. Minimizing customers' pain will usually be far more successful than attempting to create delight among already unhappy customers. Because satisfaction-maintaining attributes are core attributes, customers are likely to consider a business's performance to be the price of entry in the marketplace. Therefore, it is imperative that acceptable levels of performance (performance thresholds) be reached before initiatives are undertaken to delight customers. Delighting customers requires first that they are not dissatisfied with the delivery of their core needs.

• **Customer Delight Principle 3:** For delight-creating attributes, it is imperative to identify the performance level at which positive changes result in significant improvements in overall satisfaction. This requires identifying both the responsiveness of attributes to change (the curvilinearity of the relationship) and the position on the curve dictated by current levels of performance. Therefore it becomes critical to determine the performance level necessary to traverse the delight threshold at which positive performance produces customer delight.

A key first step in this process is to identify the relationship of the performance of the various attributes on customer satisfaction and delight, which requires identifying the asymmetry of the relationship for virtually all attributes.

However, invoking an asymmetric and nonlinear view of the attribute performance and satisfaction interface raises some practical issues. Specifically, how should we display asymmetric attribute importance and performance in a two-dimensional space such that frontline managers easily understand it? An example from a mutual fund context is instructive in this regard. In this particular instance, management was interested in examining key drivers of customer satisfaction and delight with mutual fund advisers.

The relative strength of the relationship between overall satisfaction and each attribute is shown in Figure 4.4. The weight of each attribute when expectations are not met is shown as a shaded bar to the left, and as a solid bar to the right when expectations are exceeded. A dummy variable regression was conducted to ascertain if the impact of performing below expectations was different from the impact of performing above expectations.

What's interesting here is the fact that some attributes are delight-creating attributes (for example, I feel like a valued customer) while others are satisfaction-maintaining attributes (can solve problems in one call/visit, for example). More specifically, "soft" attributes related to relationship building are delight-creating, while "core" attributes related to the operational aspects of the service provision are satisfaction-maintaining.

Delight-creating attributes with low delight levels and satisfaction-maintaining attributes with high dissatisfaction levels were identified as action priorities. On the former, a firm should take steps to increase pos-

Figure 4.4 *Asymmetric Key-Driver Analysis—Satisfaction with Mutual Fund Adviser*

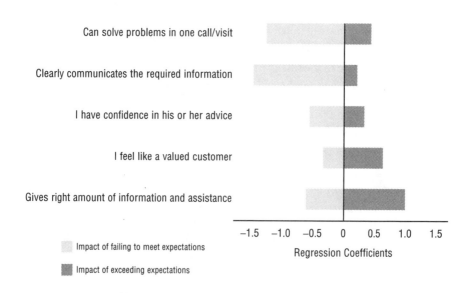

itive performance, and on the latter the appropriate strategy is to implement a "zero-tolerance" initiative, ensuring delivery levels are maintained.

As this example shows, the asymmetric relationships can be meaningfully translated into action plans for a firm. This translation requires, however, a new perspective for analyzing customer satisfaction data.

Not Everyone Is the Same

Compounding managers' difficulties in properly responding to this new view is the matter of differences among customers. The nature and extent of the asymmetry for certain attributes is likely to vary for different groups or segments of customers. Many bases for segmentation exist, and each can impact how attributes are classified. Customers' lifetimes and their felt loyalties are two segmentation bases that most certainly will impact how variables are classified.

A variety of recent reports document how customers differ in their responses to change in attribute performance, satisfaction, and retention. For example, research on airline passengers found that quality of meals was equally important among all segments. However, comfort was eight times more important among business travelers who more frequently took long international trips. Similarly, researchers found that among theater-goers, the importance of attributes such as quality of the actors and quality of the theater varied depending on whether the customers were attending a single performance or were season subscribers. Other research has found that, in determining overall satisfaction with computer software, an attribute such as documentation was more important among novice users than experts. Meanwhile, reliability and capability were more important for expert users than for beginners. Finally, research has found that the importance of various attributes of a hotel stay differed based on customers' ethnic background. For instance, Western travelers placed higher importance on pleasant and functional guestrooms than Asian travelers. Asian travelers, on the other hand, rated customized and personalized service as more important than Western travelers.

Failure to consider segment-specific differences may lead a firm to optimize performance on the wrong attribute for a targeted segment. Worse yet, by failing to consider segment-specific differences firms may conclude that, on average, an attribute is not important when in fact its importance to a particular segment has been artificially masked. And, it is entirely possible that the same attribute could be satisfaction-maintaining for one segment and delight-creating for another. Therefore, when determining attribute importance, attention should also be paid to segment-wise differences in the nature of the attribute.

Time Changes Everything

Whether an attribute is satisfaction-maintaining or delight-creating will likely change over time. Time is important in two respects. First, one should consider how much time has elapsed since the attribute was introduced to the market or category. When a performance attribute is first introduced, it is typically delight-creating: cup holders in cars, telephones or video-on-demand on airplanes, access to account information via the Internet, or a sense of humor in an accountant. Over time, however, as more competitors match the attribute, it will no longer surprise customers. Customers tend to take familiar performance attributes for granted, pushing these variables into the satisfaction-maintaining category.

Industry structure is likely to affect the speed with which attributes migrate from the delight-creating to the satisfaction-maintaining category. The more competitive a market or category is, the faster the migration. In order to optimize resources and maximize satisfaction, firms should track closely this migration of key attributes.

Second, whether an attribute is satisfaction-maintaining or delight-creating may also depend on the customer's tenure (length of relationship) with the company. For instance, among customers of a mutual fund company, trust and confidence in the adviser is a delight-creating attribute for customers in the initial stages of relationship with the firm. However, as the relationship matures, trust and confidence evolves into a satisfaction-maintaining attribute. As it has been satisfactorily experienced, it becomes expected. Failure to consider such timing differences may lead a firm to treat both newly acquired and loyal customers the same. Practicality, on the other hand, may dictate that different attributes be stressed at different times in a customer's relationship.

Delight Progression Interface 2: Customer Satisfaction Leads to Customer Retention

Customer satisfaction matters little if it doesn't ultimately impact customer behavior. As a result, there has been an increasing emphasis on

Maximally Creating Delight

- Performance attributes can be classified into different types according to their uniqueness, whether or not customers expect to receive them, and their impact on satisfaction.

- Once performance attributes are classified, Customer Delight Principles 1 and 2 provide guidelines for driving satisfaction improvement by managing performance of these attributes according to their type.

- Caution must be exercised because the classification of performance attributes is likely to change over time and across customer groupings or segments.

demonstrably interfacing customer satisfaction to drivers of business performance. We applaud this movement to accountability, as too many programs of the past seem to have been adopted and maintained in the complete absence of supporting information. The primary interface between customer satisfaction and profits is through customer retention. In fact, research has found that for a service industry, a one-unit change in overall satisfaction produces a 6 percent change in "likelihood of continuing to use" scores. Like the majority of the studies, however, the asymmetric and nonlinear aspects of the interface were not further explored.

Figure 4.5 shows a typical pattern of asymmetry observed in the Swedish Customer Satisfaction Barometer (SCSB) and American Customer Satisfaction Index (ACSI) databases. These are national databases that are constructed at the University of Michigan.[3] The data validate that the interface between satisfaction and repurchase intent (an attitudinal indicator of retention) is asymmetric: small improvements overcoming dissatisfaction have a greater impact on repurchase intent than small improvements in mere satisfaction. The interface is nonlinear in that the impact of satisfaction on repurchase intent is greater at the extremes.

Figure 4.5 *Satisfaction-Retention Link*

What accounts for the postulated nonlinearity and asymmetry in the interface between satisfaction and repurchase? When repurchasing, satisfied customers are less motivated to engage in search; they are content to consider a smaller set of brands than dissatisfied customers. Delighted customers have little incentive to even consider other brands. On the contrary, by changing brands they risk losing some of their current delight. As customers cross the threshold from Merely Satisfied to Delighted, the number of competitive firms that a customer will consider drops dramatically. Competing brands are ignored in favor of the one that has delighted the buyer in the past.

As the customer's consideration set narrows, reducing the number of acceptable alternatives, the likelihood of retaining the customer increases correspondingly. For example, an airline customer who is Merely Satisfied is more likely to consider several airlines as viable alternatives, but a delighted customer is so pleased with his or her current carrier that there is no reason to consider other carriers at all. Moving in the other direction, as dissatisfaction increases, customers are more likely to seek out and examine a wider array of alternatives. In other words, the number of acceptable competitors steadily increases as a customer's dissatisfaction increases. Eventually, customer retention declines sharply as more and more customers exclude from further consideration the brand or firm that is creating their dissatisfaction.

As seen in the SCSB and ACSI databases, the shape of the relationship between satisfaction and repurchase, and especially the elbows, or points at which customers cross the threshold and become either "customers for life" or "customers nevermore," varies enormously across industries. Some of the most typical factors influencing the shape of the interface between satisfaction and repurchase are listed in Table 4.1.

Without a full understanding of the shape of the relationship, most practitioners act as if the satisfaction-retention interface were linear and symmetric by default. This assumption has unfortunate (and costly) consequences. The impact of satisfaction on retention for changes in the middle range of the satisfaction continuum—the Zone of Mere Satisfaction—will be systematically overestimated. The behavioral changes due to slight increases in satisfaction will be far less than anticipated, possibly causing some to question the efficacy of satisfaction improvement as a business initiative. Conversely, the impact of satisfaction on retention in the extreme regions will be underestimated. Underestimating the effect of these changes leads to missed opportunities to delight customers on one end and losing customers altogether on the other.

Research into automobile customers' repurchases found that, using a linear estimation, the impact of changing satisfaction from a score of 4 to 5 was underestimated by 64 percent! Similarly, information concerning physicians' satisfaction levels was compared to their prescribing behaviors. Results showed that using a linear approach would have underestimated the impact of delighting physicians by 31 percent. This represented a financial loss of $150 per physician.

Likewise, a linear approach underestimates the severity of dissatisfaction. For instance, research in the automobile industry found that a linear analysis of the data incorrectly suggested that somewhat dissatisfied

Table 4.1 *Factors Influencing the Shape of the Link Between Satisfaction and Repurchase*

- Aggressiveness of competition

- Existence and degree of switching barriers

- Ability of customers to accurately assess quality

- Customers' level of risk aversion

customers had a higher repurchase rate than completely dissatisfied customers. In reality, somewhat dissatisfied customers were just as likely as completely dissatisfied customers to leave the company's franchise! In this case, dissatisfaction acted as a binary, threshold event.

The assumption of linearity is most dangerous in the relatively flat Zone of Mere Satisfaction. It is our belief that numerous firms became disenchanted with satisfaction improvement initiatives when they failed to observe benefits as a result of modest increases in satisfaction scores. Customers whose overall satisfaction level falls within the Zone of Mere Satisfaction are unlikely to display dramatic increases in loyalty behavior in response to small improvements in their satisfaction. Moreover, they will continue to engage in considerable switching among brands or firms. They will appear significantly different from customers who have been moved up to the Zone of Delight and whose purchasing behavior is not simply monogamous but downright exclusive. As a result, a firm whose customers fall primarily in the Zone of Mere Satisfaction and continue to defect while displaying modest satisfaction may mistakenly conclude that customer satisfaction is an unimportant prerequisite for retention in its industry or current situation.

If, in this case, resources are drained away from programs aimed at improving customer satisfaction, serious consequences are likely to ensue. First, a large proportion of customers are likely to slip into the Zone of Pain. This will cause them to drop the product or service from consideration. Second, the firm is unlikely ever to realize the benefits of delighting customers, giving its competitors yet another opportunity. Such a misread can mark the beginning of a downward spiral as competitors lock in their own delighted customers, reaping the benefits of their loyalty and reinvesting the proceeds in attracting and creating more delighted customers. For the firm that reduces its commitment to customer delight, it will become increasingly difficult and costly to attract customers away from competitors.

Managerial Consequences

Companies often look in the wrong places for payback from customer satisfaction. Delighted customers will certainly buy more, increase their "share of wallet" to those firms delighting them, and tell others to deal with these firms. But the major payback from delighted customers is longer lifetimes. This point gives us our fourth principle:

• **Customer Delight Principle 4:** The most profound profit impact from increased satisfaction will manifest itself in terms of increased retention rates of customers. Again, however, the relationship between satisfaction and either expressed (attitudinal) or observed retention will be curvilinear not linear.

Mediating Factors

As with the interface between attribute performance and satisfaction, combining the above insights with a segmentation scheme can be of enormous help. First, customer segments may vary with respect to how their retention rates change in response to changes in satisfaction level. Second, the nature of the "retention curve" may vary by segment. And third, the cost of increasing satisfaction may understandably vary by customer segment.

The importance of combining segmentation with satisfaction-retention analysis is illustrated in several recent studies. For instance, some recent studies show that among customers of a single firm, retention is much more responsive to changes in satisfaction ratings for certain customer groups than others. The key is ensuring that the segments are identifiable, distinct, have widespread support among managers, and are compatible with the firm's overall strategy.

Finally, firms should consider the impact of competition on the satisfaction-retention interface. Two firms operating in different industries may have identical satisfaction levels, yet the relationship between customer satisfaction and retention may be quite different. If one firm faces more aggressive competition, the relationship between satisfaction and retention will be weaker. In particular, both inflection points on the satisfaction-retention curve shift to the right, shrinking the Zone of Delight and widening the Zone of Pain. To better assess the impact of satisfaction on retention, firms must account for the attractiveness of alternative providers in addition to and in comparison with the drawing power of their own offerings.

These two mediating considerations give us our fifth principle:

• **Customer Delight Principle 5:** Review your customer database to identify groups or segments that will respond quite differently to satisfaction initiatives. Consider that the nature and aggressiveness of competition in one's category will also mediate the responsiveness of customers to satisfaction initiatives.

Managing Increases in Customer Retention

• Improving customer satisfaction increases the likelihood of a customer staying with the firm and repurchasing the firm's products or services, increasing his or her lifetime as a customer. This is the most tangible result of increasing the satisfaction of your customers.

• The satisfaction-retention relationship (as the performance-satisfaction relationship before it) is both nonlinear and asymmetric. Firms must recognize that this means payback for small improvements from midrange satisfaction scores will be less than expected, and returns on changes in the extreme ranges of both high and low satisfaction will be more pronounced than expected.

Delight Progression Interface 3: Customer Retention Leads to Profitability

Now let us consider how retention is related to profitability by examining how retaining a customer benefits a firm. Higher customer retention means a base of customers who buy more frequently and in greater volumes, are more prone to try other offerings by the firm ("cross-buying"), generally require lower maintenance, and become less sensitive to the outreach of competitors, thus increasing revenues while lowering the cost of marketing and sales by engaging in positive word-of-mouth recommendations. Therefore, retained customers are a revenue-producing asset for the firm.

Revenue from retained customers, however, comes at a cost. Profit may be negative over the first several purchase cycles due to the cost of acquiring the customer. Customers may only become profitable over time. Customer retention is therefore a net present value proposition (i.e., the current value of future revenue justifies the cost of investment).

Though many models have been developed to assess customer value, their basic logic is the same: a firm must first spend resources to acquire customers (acquisition cost) and then to cultivate them (maintenance cost). Balancing these costs is the revenue stream (revenues) generated by a customer. The contribution to the bottom line, then, is

cumulative revenue – (acquisition cost + cumulative maintenance cost)

The acquisition cost is an upfront expenditure, while the revenue comes over a long period of time—hence the importance of customer retention.[4]

Firms that keep acquiring new customers but are unable to retain them are unlikely to see positive bottom-line results. The revenue stream from a retained customer is lost to the firm when the customer leaves. The firm not only loses sales but also the benefits of retained customers, such as lower servicing and marketing costs. The loyal customer has to be replaced (at a high acquisition premium) by a new customer who initially buys less frequently and in smaller quantities (lower revenues), requires more service (higher service cost), and is less likely to recruit new customers (higher marketing costs). To make the same level of sales, a firm with a low retention rate must incur higher costs. Consequently, the deleterious impact of losing a customer can be much greater than the benefit reaped from retaining a customer. In addition, the competitive nature of categories amplifies this asymmetry, as firms with relatively low customer satisfaction are unlikely to attract many delighted, loyal customers from their rivals.

The impact of customer satisfaction on profitability is not only asymmetric but also nonlinear (see Figure 4.6). The shape of this relationship suggests that extravagant expenditures to increase customer retention may eventually lead to overspending. There are diminishing returns to efforts to continuously increase satisfaction and, therefore, retention. This leads to our sixth principle:

• **Customer Delight Principle 6:** Profit from improving the retention rate of a firm's customers is experienced over the long term only. In similar fashion as the other two stages of the Delight Progression, profit will respond to changes in retention in a curvilinear manner, with the greatest responsiveness at the extremes of retention. Customer lifetimes and lifetime values offer the most definitive method for tracking improvement.

Delight Isn't Free

The goal of increasing customer satisfaction implies offering products and services with more and better features made available in a greater variety of combinations, while more attention is paid to customers by employees. These improved features, added varieties, and increased attention are all cost intensive. Net-net, the cost of boosting customer satisfaction usually rises at an increasing rate. Even though costs may decline for a time due to fewer defects and lower warranty costs, as with all production functions, diminishing returns to such efforts are likely and costs will eventually begin to rise.

For example, technology providing improvements in the precision of manufactured components may be unavailable. Increasing inspection on an assembly line may be impractical. Customers may cease to notice further refinements in reliability. Costs of hiring and training qualified service personnel may become prohibitive. After a certain point, the increase in costs will outweigh the beneficial effects of further customer satisfaction. Therefore, overall, there are diminishing returns when relating satisfaction and delight to profitability.

A similar logic operates when relating customer retention to profitability. This happens because, from a given pool of customers, not all customers are as attractive to keep in terms of revenue generation. (Customer-retention efforts are most rewarding when directed at high-value, low-cost customers, a small proportion of any business's customers.) Fur-

Figure 4.6 Retention-Profit Link

Customer Retention

Note: The dotted line represents a linear approximation of the nonlinear relationship shown.

ther, successive acquisition of customers is likely to be more expensive. Thus, as a firm keeps acquiring more and more customers, the quality of the acquired customers may decline. The new customers will incur higher maintenance costs and will produce lower revenue, resulting in diminishing returns. The key is to operate at a steady state and focus on acquiring and keeping the "right" customers, rather than just blindly expanding the total customer base.

Managerial Consequences

Take, for example, a leading mutual fund company that found varying levels of retention and profitability among different customer segments. Based on these differences, the firm ascertained the differential cost of attracting new customers into each of these segments. More importantly, by calculating the cost of maintaining customers in each segment and the revenue those customers generated, the firm was able to calculate the differential profitability rates for each segment. In one segment it was able to recoup all of its up-front costs of recruiting customers within a reasonably short 6 years, while in another segment it would have taken the firm more than 230 years to do the same thing! Needless to say, the firm decided it would not be in its best interest to pursue customer retention

---

Managing Increases in Profitability

- Profit from improved retention is experienced in the long-term only, and customers become increasingly more profitable as their lifetimes lengthen. Establishing a procedure for calculating and then consistently monitoring customer lifetime value is one of the most beneficial activities that a company can undertake.

- Just as in the previous two stages of the Delight Progression, the retention-profit relationship is curvilinear and asymmetric. Firms must focus on not overspending to keep customers and on identifying those customers they really need to retain.

for the latter segment. As this example demonstrates, firms should assess the retention-profitability interface separately for each segment and then decide on an optimal resource allocation strategy for optimizing retention and profitability.

Summary

The interfaces in the Delight Progression do work. Specifically, firms that manage to create delight enjoy commensurate profits. However, it is becoming increasingly clear that achieving this objective requires replacing the traditional view of the satisfaction-profit chain as linear and symmetric with a new perspective (such as Delight Progression) that recognizes the greater complexity in these interfaces.

In our Delight Progression, the interfaces between stages are not only asymmetric and nonlinear but also subject to contextual complexities such as customer demographics, the competitive environment, and temporal differences. Thus, it is imperative to develop a sophisticated system that recognizes, understands, and incorporates these rich and unique facets. Every implementation is different and needs to be customized to the particular firm, the particular product, and the particular market segment. The process, though painstaking, creates customer delight and generates company profits.

Chapter Key Notes

In this chapter we have established the six principles of customer delight.

Customer Delight Principle 1: Performance attributes (the way customers judge the adequacy of products, services, and suppliers) may be divided into at least two kinds: satisfaction-maintaining attributes and delight-creating attributes.

Customer Delight Principle 2: To maximize satisfaction with satisfaction-maintenance attributes, one must first insure against negative performance.

Customer Delight Principle 3: To maximize satisfaction with delight-creating attributes, it is imperative to identify the performance level at which improvements result in significant increases in overall satisfaction.

Customer Delight Principle 4: Improved retention rates are the primary conduit between increased performance, which creates heightened satisfaction, and profitability.

Customer Delight Principle 5: Segments of customers within a firm's customer base and the aggressiveness of competitors will mitigate or exacerbate the responsiveness of customers to improvements in performance.

Customer Delight Principle 6: Realizing profit from improvements in retention rates is a long-term process. Firms should commit to measuring and tracking customer lifetimes and lifetime values to best assess the effects of their Delight Progression.

Notes

1. Statistically, this is accomplished by a variety of covariance methods, such as correlation, regression, or structural equation models. For a review of methods, see "Determining Attribute Importance" by R. Hanson in *Quirk's Marketing Research Review* (October 1992).

2. For an explanation of the traditional quadrant chart, see *Improving Your Measurement of Customer Satisfaction* by Terry Vavra.

3. For details, see "A National Customer Satisfaction Barometer: The Swedish Experience," by Claes Fornell in *Journal of Marketing* or "Customer Satisfaction, Market Share, and Profitability: Findings from Sweden" by Eugene W. Anderson, Claes Fornell, and Donald R. Lehmann in *Journal of Marketing*.

4. For examples of this equation at work, see "Manage Market by the Customer Equity Test" by Robert C. Blattberg and John Deighton in *Harvard Business Review* or *Customer Connections: New Strategies for Growth* by R. E. Wayland and P. M. Cole.

5

The Role of Employees

On April 2, 1982, the War of the Falkland Islands began with a successful invasion by Argentinian forces. Britain responded by sending its finest soldiers to recapture the islands. Ten weeks after the invasion, Argentinian soldiers surrendered to British forces.

At one point in the fighting, three hundred Argentinians were retreating before the Scots Guards when they encountered an advance patrol of fighters with a fearsome reputation. Immediately they ran back to surrender to the Scots Guards. The troops the Argentinians so feared, however, were not British subjects but citizens of Nepal. They represented the 1/7th Gurkha Rifles unit of the British army.

Before the 1/7th had left its base for the Falkland Islands, the press had taken a series of photographs of the Gurkha soldiers preparing for war, including some that showed the Gurkhas sharpening and brandishing their long, curved kukri battle knives. Not long afterward, stories about the "wicked Gurkhas" appeared in the Argentinian media. Clearly their reputation worked to their advantage. "They knew we were coming and they feared us," said Lieutenant-Colonel David Morgan, commandant of the 1/7th Gurkha Rifles. "Of course, I think they had every reason to fear us."

The Gurkhas, sturdy Nepalese mountain men, have served in the British army since the mid–nineteenth century. They have fought the enemies of Britain, with several hundred thousand fighting alongside the British during the first and second world wars. Their bravery in numerous battles has brought them fame and admiration.

Although Nepal was never a British colony and as a sovereign nation owes no allegiance to Britain, around 70,000 Gurkhas apply for 250 spots in the British army each year. Every Gurkha soldier has been a volunteer, and in many cases their fathers and grandfathers have served before them.

Field-Marshal Lord Slim, who served with the Gurkhas as a regimental officer and commanded them as a general in battle, effused tremendous praise and appreciation of the Gurkha soldiers:

> The Almighty created in the Gurkha an ideal infantryman, indeed an ideal rifleman, brave, tough, patient, adaptable, skilled in fieldcraft, intensely proud of his military record and unswerving loyalty. Add to this his honesty in word and deed, his parade perfection, and his unquenchable cheerfulness, then service with Gurkhas is for any soldier an immense satisfaction.

The Front Line

To the customer, the face of the company is not the CEO. It is the front-line personnel who make that all-important contact with the customer. It matters little if the company's policies and procedures are designed to delight customers if the people charged with carrying them out fail to deliver for the customer.

Consistently delivering delight demands effectively managing relationships with customers. And close, long-term relationships are only possible with long-term employees. Most firms, however, are unable to match the recruiting success of the British army with regard to the devotion and productivity of its Gurkha units. As a result, companies that embark on a service strategy often, understandably, make a concerted effort to focus on improving their employee relations as well. The management logic is simple: Customer relations mirror employee relations. Without question there is some evidence to support this often-used truism.

A survey of more than 7,500 workers found that more than half considered themselves committed to their employers. Shareholders of these employers received on average a 112 percent return on their investment over three years. For those employees who indicated average or below average commitment, however, the average return to shareholders was 76 percent.

Such evidence supports the widely held belief that employee satisfaction is part of a virtuous cycle leading to improved customer satisfaction and better business outcomes. In fact, virtually every model designed to explain the chain of effects of service on financial performance from beginning to end presumes a critical link in the chain to be employee satisfaction.

But exactly how does employee satisfaction lead to customer satisfaction and delight? Is it necessary to have delighted employees to have delighted customers? Should one go to the extreme advocated by Hal Rosenbluth in his admittedly overstated book title, *The Customer Comes Second*?

Because of the assumed impact on performance, for the past thirty years employee commitment has been one of the most popular research areas in industrial psychology and organizational behavior. However, counter to conventional wisdom, researchers have been unable to confirm a relationship between employee commitment and business performance. While some studies have found a relationship, other studies have been unable to do the same. As one team of researchers noted, "Although higher levels of commitment may relate to improved job performance in some situations . . . the present findings suggest that commitment has very little direct influence on performance in most instances."

The lack of a relationship between business outcomes and employee satisfaction seems counterintuitive. We have all had experiences as consumers in which a disgruntled employee has caused us to be dissatisfied (through rudeness, indifference, ineptitude, etc.). Likewise, we have all had experiences in which an employee transformed an ordinary or even potentially disastrous experience into a delightful one through extraordinary action and palpable concern for us.

With such a rich history of research on the subject, why isn't there conclusive evidence of a relationship? Clearly, there must be a more complex set of factors governing the relationship between employee satisfaction, customer satisfaction, and business performance.

The service management faculty at the Harvard Business School suggests that the strength of the relationship may be contingent upon four elements relevant to employees: capability, satisfaction, loyalty, and productivity. These four elements are thought to directly influence customer satisfaction. The reasoning plays out like this:

- Capable employees can deliver high-value service to customers. This requires that employees have the training, tools, procedures, and rules necessary to deliver good service.

- Satisfied employees are more likely to treat customers better than their dissatisfied counterparts.

- Loyal employees are more willing to suppress short-term interests for the long-term benefit of the organization. As such, they provide superior service to customers. Furthermore, loyal employees stay with the organization longer, reducing the cost of turnover and its negative impact on service quality.

- Productive employees have the potential to raise the value of a firm's offerings to its customers. Greater productivity can lower costs of operations, which means prices can be lowered.

Besides the traditionally emphasized elements of employee satisfaction and loyalty, we have the added dimensions of capability and productivity. Intuitively we know that the combination of these elements makes for a better employee and a better experience for the customer.

Employee Capability

Without question, no matter how satisfied or loyal a firm's employees, if they are not capable of serving the needs of customers, then customers will not be delighted, much less satisfied. We've all heard the common employee lament, "I wish I could help you, but I can't change company policy."

The importance of employee capability has implications for hiring the "right" people as well. This might mean hiring on the basis of not only technical skills and experience but also more personal characteristics. For example, the Olive Garden restaurant chain prefers to hire prospective managers with strong ties to the communities in which they develop business. Likewise, research by J. Weiner and J. C. Mowen has shown that salespeople who are perceived as similar to the customers they serve tend to be more successful. The same research also proposes that employees be screened for social abilities that promote long-term interpersonal relationships. Nordstrom exemplifies this approach with its "hire the smile" policy, believing it easier to teach employees to sell than to be pleasant to others.

Establishing relationships with customers demands long-term service from employees. It is imperative that firms recognize the importance of personal relationships between employees and customers. For instance, research in the banking industry in 1996 revealed that many customers become dissatisfied when personnel are switched from one branch to another. Therefore, it is important to design jobs that encourage employees to stay. While compensation will be a factor, so too will job-advancement opportunities and the ability to continue to learn.

It is often a delicate balance to provide the opportunities for advancement necessary to make jobs attractive to employees while maintaining a familiar relationship for customers. Employees need to feel that, through their current position, they can attain their career objectives, which often include transfers to other locations or departments within an organization. But just as promoting your best salesman out of the field can have a deleterious impact on sales, so too can improperly thought out succession plans of employees who touch the customer.

One advantage of long-term employee relationships is that long-term employees justify a greater investment in training, which improves employee capability while fulfilling the employees' needs to continuously learn and grow. Robert T. Herres, CEO of USAA notes:

> We want to keep employees when we shift to new processes. They come with assets like loyalty, commitment to customers, and understanding of our culture and our mission. We've therefore struck a bargain: we'll provide them with the training they need if they're willing to do their part and invest in self-development and education. CEOs need to accept the challenge of retraining their employees just as they retool their machinery and equipment.

The importance of capability requires that employees are equipped with the right tools. Consistently delighting customers requires having in place systems that allow employees to best serve customers. We've all experienced a "crashed" computer that prevented an employee from adequately assisting us. All too often, however, managers want to focus exclusively on the "friendly" and "knowledgeable" components of employee skills needed to delight customers while giving short shrift to fundamental process improvements, such as computer upgrades, that would make it easier for employees to actually perform their jobs.

But customer delight is a function of a company's total offering to customers. The quality of a company's products and its service quality are intertwined to produce delight. Simply having knowledgeable, friendly employees will not solve fundamental product or process problems. As many retailers have learned, there is rarely a right way to tell the customer, "We don't have your product."

Employee Productivity

When considering employee capability, employee satisfaction, and employee loyalty, it is logical to believe that all of these elements can be positively correlated to one another and to customer satisfaction. However, it is easy to imagine how employee *productivity* could be positively correlated to customer satisfaction but negatively correlated to employee satisfaction and employee loyalty. (Without employee capability, there would be no way to please customers.)

Take the case of Internet retailer Amazon.com. Amazon is well known for its high level of customer service and user satisfaction relative to its competitors. A key element of this success derives from the rapid response it is able to give customers to their inquiries. But, to quote Mark Leibovich in his article in the *Washington Post*:

> This promise of speed rests heavily on rote-work employees—the men and women who spend their days and nights boxing books at Amazon's distribution centers, and those who answer E-mail. . . . So it's out of necessity—or desperation—that Amazon's customer-service managers push their employees hard.

The title of the article, "At Amazon.com, Service Workers Without a Smile," hammers home the fact that employee productivity can make for happy customers and unhappy employees.

Similarly, Nordstrom, in creating almost legendary customer appreciation practically burnt out its associates and triggered numerous legal problems for itself. At issue was the chain's insistence that associates write postpurchase notes of appreciation to their customers. The customers were flattered by the unexpected notes; the associate's were distressed at having to write them.

Productivity-based improvements in service also tend to require a tradeoff in quality. Seldom can service firms do both well. Research has found that service companies that pursued a high service quality and high productivity strategy were less profitable than those that chose to be either high service only or high productivity only. Therefore, if productivity improvements are the primary means of driving delight, managers need to realize that doing this successfully requires walking a tightrope. The potential for dissatisfying employees might make any gains short-lived as customer-service personnel seek employment elsewhere.

Focus First on Customers

The issue is not whether it is better to have capable, satisfied, loyal, and productive employees. Even if there were no connection to customer satisfaction, there is a positive relationship between these elements and employee retention. The savings that accompanies reducing employee turnover (for instance, less recruiting, less training, and so on) will almost always justify minimizing employee dissatisfaction. But revenue is driven by customers. And without question, customer delight is paramount. It matters little if you have capable, satisfied, loyal, and productive employees if your customers are not delighted. The fundamental rule of business is to satisfy customer needs and wants at a profit. Failure to meet this rule makes employee satisfaction a moot point, as the early 2000 demise of so many E-commerce sites clearly demonstrates.

Once you have determined *what* delights customers, then you can decide *how* to delight them. The first step is to align processes around customer needs and to align people and resources to support these processes. But as processes are aligned, it is essential to inform employees why the changes are being made. Change is upsetting, and often change in companies is ill-defined and subject to reversal. Failure to explain to employees the basis for the changes being made places those changes in jeopardy. But if the changes are introduced as being driven by the desire to delight customers, acceptance could be improved. Employees should value customer-centered initiatives; they have to conclude their jobs will be made easier with happier customers.

This transformation does not necessarily require delighted employees. It does require satisfied employees who are committed to delighting customers. It also requires having the right employees in place.

According to Robert Spector and Patrick McCarthy, authors of *The Nordstrom Way*, Nordstrom refuses to acquire other retailers and convert them into a Nordstrom store for fear of acquiring employees with bad habits. Likewise, many firms that have transformed their companies through customer delight have been faced with the reality that not all members of their current staff were capable of following or wanted to follow this path. To quote the president of Roche Diagnostics, Carlo Medici, who faced this situation head on, "You have to be ready to take a hard stance and accept some issues in the short term. But you hire the right caliber of people." (See Chapter 8 for more on Roche Diagnostics.)

The importance of this commitment cannot be overstated. As Ray Kordupleski, former customer satisfaction director for AT&T, observed:

> Studying customer satisfaction and dissatisfaction over the years, I have found that no one person in any organization can totally satisfy a customer. But any one person can totally dissatisfy a customer. Completely satisfying a customer requires totally focused and aligned people.

Summary

Delivering delight consistently demands developing long-term relationships with customers, which demands long-term relationships with employees. Research, however, has been unable to conclusively demonstrate a direct relationship between employee satisfaction and business outcomes.

It has been proposed that employee satisfaction represents one of four employee-related elements that are thought to influence customer satisfaction: capability, satisfaction, loyalty, and productivity. However, this does not mean that having employees who are capable, satisfied, loyal, and productive will create customer delight. It is necessary to focus first on customers and then to work with employees to implement processes that will make it possible to delight customers. The key is having satisfied employees who are committed to customer delight.

Chapter Key Notes

- Employee satisfaction alone is not enough to generate customer delight.
- Four elements relevant to employees are believed to be important to delighting customers:

  1. Capable employees can deliver high-value service to customers.
  2. Satisfied employees are more likely to treat customers better than their dissatisfied counterparts.

3. Loyal employees are more willing to suppress short-term interests for the long-term benefit of the organization.
4. Productive employees have the potential to raise the value of a firm's offerings to its customers.

- The first step is to align processes around customer needs and to align people and resources to support these processes.

6

The New Business Reality

This chapter was written by Roland T. Rust in conjunction with the authors. Roland T. Rust holds the David Bruce Smith Chair in Marketing at the Robert H. Smith School of Business at the University of Maryland. He has won best-article awards for articles in Marketing Science, Journal of Marketing, Journal of Advertising, *and* Journal of Retailing, *and he has received career achievement awards from the American Statistical Association, the American Academy of Advertising, and the University of North Carolina at Chapel Hill.*

IF ONE ACCEPTS the importance of delight in making a business or enterprise successful over the long run, then one must also be concerned about creating it within today's economy. The fact of the matter is, despite the importance of delight, today's economic situation defies providing excellent service. On a CNN newscast in April 2000, various managers of service businesses expressed these concerns:

- How can I deliver good service when most of my customer-contact people don't give a damn?
- I'd like to be more choosy in hiring, but the truth is, I have to hire virtually anyone I can get!
- I have to offer even my part-time people full medical plans!

No strategy is borne or executed in a vacuum, and the customer delight principle is no less subject to the environment in which it is implemented. Today's market is far different from any of the past. It poses problems of seemingly insurmountable difficulty. Yet, some aspects of today's competitive situation are highly compatible with providing delight.

Waves of Change

Our economies and markets are in enormous upheaval. Developed global economies are radically shifting toward the service sector. Concurrent with this shift and the traumatic adaptation it requires, the seismic impact of the information revolution is rumbling through our businesses. In these challenging times, the attention of several writers has focused on what is being labeled "the new economy" and how it seems to be changing the rules of productivity, growth, and profitability—how it is changing the very ways we conduct business.

What often is not mentioned nor even realized is how the information revolution and the shift to the service sector are both facets of the same transformation. The information revolution, and the new economy that results from it, are demanding a new, service-focused approach from management. What's more, a new, coherent set of management principles follows naturally from how the economy has begun to work. Understanding these principles is critical to realizing both the importance of delivering customer delight and the substantial challenges such a goal will exact in the new economy.

We believe that embracing the new economy will require a profound shift in how companies are managed. In fact, many of the currently popular managerial practices will be (or already are) obsolete! The central phenomenon driving this shift is the rapidly increasing productivity of information technology, which in turn leads to the overwhelming dominance of the service economy and to revenue growth rather than cost reduction as the winning business strategy. The expanding economy places a premium on retaining both high-value customers and dedicated employees, reversing trends of the recent past in which current customers were taken for granted and employees were underappreciated and often "downsized" out of their jobs.

Businesses must adapt to this rapidly evolving market. The marketing department is one of the primary corporate departments that can help effect this change, and it needs to step forward with its capabilities to assist the evolution. In general, businesses must become three things:

1. More "outside-focused," because that is where revenues come from

2. More long-term–oriented, because long-term customer relationships are the key to revenues

3. More focused on service excellence, because delighting customers is the key to long-term success

While each of these ideas has been proposed individually, the newly productive information economy is actually a coherent, unifying theme that weaves all of these managerial themes together. This new economy demands a management style dedicated to motivating employees to offer service that actually *exceeds* customer expectations, elevating customers to a state of delight. (See Figure 6.1.)

The Productivity Turnaround

When the information revolution started, roughly around 1960, it was widely believed that information technologies such as computers would quickly make service more productive. It came as a shock and a surprise that for many years this was not the case. In contrast, with the introduction of the quality revolution (roughly 1980 in the United States), manufacturing productivity grew by leaps and bounds as the tools of that revolution were applied, along with reengineering and other efficiency approaches. The increases in efficiency were spearheaded by manufacturing advances made in Japan and quickly spread to the United States, western Europe, and other developed economic regions.

One of the reasons the information revolution produced no similar, immediate escalation in service productivity is that service productivity is very hard to measure and the standard government statistics that were measuring it at the time are questionable at best. Another reason is that early computerization did not actually make service more efficient, because initial computerization consumed employee time, as employees labored to get their hardware and software to work. Careful economic analyses conducted at the time inevitably concluded that computerization did not produce early paybacks.

Figure 6.1 *Managing in the New Economy*

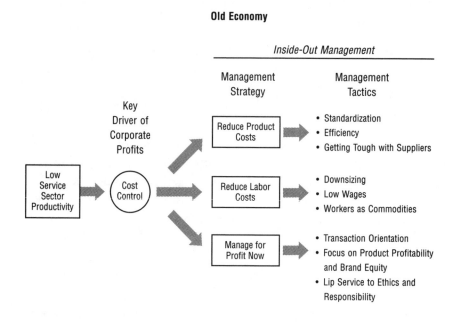

Old Economy

Inside-Out Management

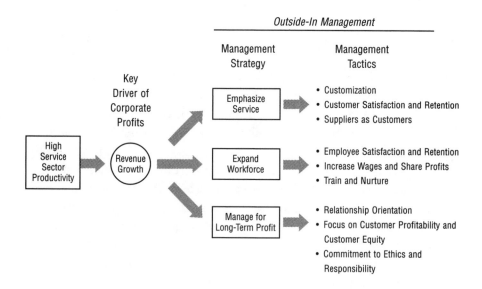

New Economy

Outside-In Management

The big turnaround was experienced in the mid-1990s. Finally the anticipated benefits of the information revolution kicked in; service productivity began to increase. And, because services account for 75 percent of the gross domestic product (GDP), this caused a great surge in productivity in the economy as a whole.

Revolution Evolution

Seems like déjà vu. We've seen similar patterns before. It took many years before the manufacturing advances of the Industrial Revolution resulted in increased productivity. We all know what happened next. Industrialization ran wild, producing impressive market successes, typified by Ford's Model T. Winning business strategies of that day had to be growth-oriented. And this high-growth environment and its subsequent demand for workers shifted the supply and demand balance in labor's favor. Many industrialists tried to battle it out with labor, but eventually the companies that fared best were the ones that treated their employees well and made peace with the labor force.

In the initial years of the new millennium, we are entering a similar period. It is interesting to note that, just as the Industrial Revolution shifted into high gear around 1900, the information revolution is shifting into high gear now, in 2001. Many of management's lessons from the second half of the Industrial Revolution are equally appropriate and helpful now.

Redefining Quality

One of the most profound ways in which management must change is in the way it defines and views quality. To a great extent the quality dogma of the 1980s still permeates business. We argue that the old view of quality must be cast aside and replaced with a new view.

The Quality-Productivity Tradeoff

"Quality is free," proclaims quality guru Philip Crosby in his book of the same name, echoing an idea that was first posed by W. Edwards Deming and the other icons of quality. They have suggested that improving quality (producing products with fewer errors) through efficiency meth-

The Impact of the New Economy

The new economy is beginning to capitalize on the productivity promises of computerization. This development will catapult customer servicing into a new realm of capabilities and benefits for customers.

ods drove down costs and ultimately delivered products that better satisfied customers, thereby increasing the likelihood of repeat business and referrals—a win-win situation. The ultimate goal of this perspective was a business model intent upon maximizing quality—and therefore customer satisfaction—while also maximizing productivity.

Deming, J. M. Juran, and the other legendary giants of quality all came of age in the manufacturing era. Recent research that uses data from the Swedish Customer Satisfaction Barometer confirms that the "quality is free" strategy does in fact work for manufacturing. However, the research also indicates that the strategy works far less well in the service sector: service companies that try to maximize quality/customer satisfaction *and* productivity at the same time tend to have lower profits. That is unfortunate, given the predominance of the service sector today in virtually all developed economies.

What Is Quality?

An intuitive understanding of this disturbing finding comes from Juran, who conceptualized two opposing kinds of quality. We refer to these as "standardization quality" and "customization quality." In manufacturing, usually the objective is to make each part coming down the assembly line exactly the same and quality is dictated by how similar the parts can be made. Quality in manufacturing, then, is characterized by *standardization*, or conforming to specifications.

In services, on the other hand, the general objective is to anticipate and cater to each customer's idiosyncratic needs and wants. In other words, quality in services is characterized by *customization*, or meeting customers' expectations.

It is easy to see that increasing quality in service-intensive businesses conceivably requires more time and attention, increasing rather than decreasing costs. This is a very different outcome from increasing quality in manufacturing, which drives down costs. These inverse relationships mean that there is an inherent tradeoff between quality/customer delight and productivity in the servicing component of most business enterprises.

Two Viable Strategies

The tradeoff between quality/customer delight and productivity implies that management must choose between having high-quality service that delights the customer and efficient, lower-quality service that increases productivity. (We will refer to these as the *high-service strategy* and the *low-cost strategy*, respectively.) Empirical research verifies that market leaders in the service sector tend to be companies that clearly choose one of these two opposing strategies.

A good example of the high-service strategy is the Ukrop's supermarket chain headquartered in Richmond, Virginia. Ukrop's markets are clearly positioned to deliver quality service. Their stores are pleasantly decorated, they offer a wide assortment of specialty foods, and as much as 40 percent of their store's space is allocated to prepared foods to go. They carry groceries to patrons' cars and offer banking services, a bakery, a florist shop, a sushi bar, and a restaurant all under one roof. Their prices are higher but so is their quality.

The low-cost strategy is exemplified by the Aldi grocery chain. In this "pallet operation," costs are reduced to the bare minimum, as customers shop in a warehouselike environment, buying in bulk. The service is minimal, but the prices are low.

The Winning Strategy

Although both high-service and low-cost are viable strategies, the former will clearly be better in a period of expansion and growth. High-service is an outside-in, customer-focused strategy that emphasizes revenue growth, while low-cost is an inside-out, internally focused strategy that emphasizes cost reduction. In an expansionary period such as the one we are entering in the early 2000s, the high-service strategy has greater prospects. In addition, high-service is more compatible with the new economy. Following is a more detailed discussion of some of the reasons high-service will be the preferred strategy.

Thinking Positively

The new economy demands an emphasis on growth, an appreciation for current customers, and a renewed respect for employees. In a very literal sense, the times call for thinking positively.

The Leaking Bucket

We've previously described how businesses have been improperly acting over the last twenty to thirty years. They have been oriented to conquering new customers—what we call "conquest marketing." The fault has been in the way marketing theory has been enacted and in the way the marketing community in general has conducted itself. In conquest marketing all marketing expenditures are focused on attracting more new customers. This is the forte of advertising, and the tremendous force of the advertising industry has been a formidable lobby against any reallocation of effort or expenditures.

The obvious problem with this operating mind-set is that all of one's future is placed in the capture of new customers, while it is quite literally the current customers that keep any enterprise in business! Because conquest marketing is so focused on increasing numbers of customers, it almost always results in a disregard for current customers, since there is no provision for effort or attention to keep them, hence the analogy of the leaking bucket. We are fixated on filling our bucket—maximizing our market share—yet, while we do so, silently but ever so constantly current customers leak out, seeking other suppliers who demonstrate more appreciation for their business, more attention to their needs.

The solution to this problem and the key to success in today's market begins with allocating attention and effort to current customers, or "retention marketing." This effort has previously been called "aftermarketing," the practice of marketing on customers *after* they've purchased a product or service. But neither should an organization commit itself 100 percent to retention marketing. Astute companies today are estab-

---

Quality and Strategies

While businesses may still choose to pursue a low-cost operating strategy in the coming years, its counter, the high-service strategy, is most compatible with the technologies and customer expectations of the new economy. Customization to customers' unique needs defines quality and is essential in producing delight.

---

lishing a balance in their marketing efforts between conquest and retention activities. An appropriate structure for the internal marketing organization can help achieve this balance.

The Sovereignty of Customers

"The customer is king!" is frequently proclaimed in business turnarounds. While this is admittedly an enthusiastic overstatement, this sort of exaggeration may be necessary to overcome some of the apathy of past years and past philosophies. The fact of the matter is, each of our customers offers an annuity of transactions or payments—what we call the customer's lifetime value. But customers are all too frequently dealt with on the basis of their current transaction. Their long-term value is disregarded, and they are delighted or dissatisfied on the basis of present, momentary considerations. All customer-contact people should be educated on the lifetime value of customers. Many in the customer-centered movement have urged employees to view a customer with a dollar amount (their lifetime value) imprinted on their forehead. With this view, the value of the customer is much more evident, and it is perhaps easier for the employee to withstand any momentary unpleasantness by recognizing how valuable the customer is to the organization in the long term. How many times have we overheard a distraught customer attempting to make his or her case with an employee stronger by saying, "I buy your product all the time . . ." In essence, the customer better understands his or her lifetime value than the employee does; otherwise some accommodation would already have been made.

More and more we need to consider the lifetime values of current customers and incorporate those values into our business and marketing planning, to maintain the outside focus. Without this knowledge, we are quite likely to fall back into the comfortable pattern of doing what's most efficient and right for ourselves.

The Importance of Dedicated Employees

As the importance of customers is more widely understood, so too will the importance of capable, dedicated, and loyal employees. Cost cutting has been the name of the game in business for almost twenty years, with companies rushing to trim fat, downsizing their workforces, and increasing their efficiencies. The heroes of the corporate world have been those that were the most ruthless. On many occasions we have seen a layoff announcement followed by a surge in a company's stock price.

But the easy cuts have all been made, which means that cost cutting has entered a period of diminishing returns, naturally leading to a search for an alternative source of profit growth. Simultaneously, the resulting increase in productivity from the information revolution makes revenue growth more and more feasible.

Supply and Demand

One of the most striking results of a growth-oriented economy is the extent to which employees become valuable. In Silicon Valley, as in all other fast-growing areas, employees are in short supply, which bids up their price. In these so-called low-supply areas, this effect is already well known—even secretaries in Silicon Valley have enough leverage to demand stock options.

This "Silicon Valley Effect" is becoming increasingly widespread, as high-growth targets and low unemployment make employees hard to find. The outcome is predictable—delighting employees in order to retain them has become a top priority. Rather than downsizing and laying off workers, companies are adopting new strategies to create loyalty in their workforce. At Federal Express, for example, new mothers are given up to a year and a half leave to spend with their new babies, and they can work however many hours they want when they return. Other workers are offered flexible hours or are given the opportunity to design their own schedule. Other companies have announced and have kept to no-layoff policies. Essentially companies are trying like mad to restore the social contract that says loyal employees will be taken care of. It is in the companies' interest to do so.

Accepting Wage Increases

One of the natural results of the employee shortage is a rise in wages. This is a simple result of supply and demand. The smart company realizes that taking too hard a line against wage increases is counterproductive. Scarcity means higher pay, and in many companies the wealth is shared to an unprecedented extent. Microsoft, with its thousands of millionaires, is a harbinger of things to come. Another way of looking at this is that CEO pay, as a multiple of average worker salary, is likely to decline again, as workers realize their economic power.

This development sounds like the resurgence of the labor movement, and that's exactly what it will be, except that this time it will not be poorly educated factory workers organizing. It will instead be relatively well educated information workers who organize. If information technology companies do not like the sound of that, then the only way out is to treat workers so well that they see no benefit in organizing. Higher wages and profit sharing throughout middle management are bound to result.

Managing Outside-In

The benefits of cutting costs come from inside an organization, but those of expanding revenue come from the outside. Because revenue expansion is becoming more important than cost cutting, the clear implication is that firms should look out to the market if they want to best compete in the new economy.

Inside-out companies are easy to spot. They focus on the product and on internal processes; they are typically efficiency-oriented. Classic inside-out companies are engineering-oriented firms in industries such as aerospace and computers. These companies tend to be more prevalent in the goods sector. A classic inside-out management approach is Total Quality Management (TQM). In TQM workers focus on increasing the efficiency of internal processes, hoping to produce cheaper and better products and trusting that the customer will eventually share the benefits.

Outside-in companies are also easy to spot. They focus on the customer, delighting him or her and in so doing building long-term relationships; they have learned to be oriented toward effectiveness. Classic

---

Valuing Customers and Employees

The new economy places higher priority on businesses properly balancing their marketing efforts between conquest of new markets and consumers and retention of those customers they already have. The key to success appears to be valuing both profitable, loyal customers and dedicated, loyal employees.

---

outside-in companies are service-oriented firms in industries such as hospitality and professional services. An outside-in orientation can be practiced in any business enterprise, though the outlook tends to be more prevalent in the service sector or where the servicing component can be made an important point of differentiation. A classic outside-in management tool is customer-value analysis, in which elements of a product or service are prioritized for delivery in proportion to their generation of customer satisfaction. In customer-value analysis the focus is on customer satisfaction, and management processes are altered to drive satisfaction ever higher.

Organizing for Revenue Growth

A revenue-growth focus implies an outside-in focus, which in turn implies a customer focus, and a customer focus requires organizing around the customer. This means that, instead of a functionally oriented organizational structure (such as marketing, finance, human resources) or a brand/product-oriented organizational structure (brand managers, for example), the outside-in focus demands account teams for large customers and segment teams for groups of smaller customers. The account team approach is well established in business-to-business marketing: an account team representing several roles and functions interacts on an ongoing basis with the customer. This approach greatly facilitates learning about the customer and strengthening the relationship with him or her over time.

Although it is not as widely applied, the same general approach is also applicable to smaller customers. In the segment team approach, a cross-functional team resembling an account team is dedicated to a particular customer segment. The team dedicates itself to learning more and more about the segment, visiting customers within the segment, and developing a deeper understanding of the segment.

With either the account team approach or the segment team approach, intimacy with the customer enables service to be tailored to the customer, and products (both physical products and service products) become increasingly targeted over time. In essence the account team member or segment team member is a customer advocate within the organization, making sure that customer delight is taken into account for corporate decision making and planning.

The Voice of the Customer

The term *voice of the customer* has come to mean an elicitation and enumeration of customer needs and requirements for the purpose of designing products. The approach arose from the Japanese method of Quality Function Deployment (QFD), also known as the "House of Quality." These methods are well established in manufacturing and have successfully been used to design service products.

However, another voice of the customer, one that is equally important, is not well captured by QFD methods, and that is the customer's opinions on service delivery and the quality of their ongoing relationship with the company. Customer responses on these topics are very different from their statements of needs and requirements from products. If customer needs and requirements determine how to plan your work, then customer response to service delivery determines how well the company works its plan. Service delivery incorporates the messy concepts of personal experience and emotion, elements that are not often reflected in lists of customer needs.

Measuring customer reaction to service delivery is generally part of the ubiquitous practice of customer satisfaction measurement. But customer satisfaction measurement is only valuable to the extent that it ties customer satisfaction to specific management processes. This enables a true outside-in approach to improvement through which the customer satisfaction responses pinpoint the management processes in which improvement will have the greatest effect on overall customer satisfaction. Fully implementing the outside-in approach demands both outside-in product design (QFD) and outside-in continual service improvement (customer delight principles). One is not a substitute for the other; they are necessary cohorts.

The New Look of Competition

In the early days of mass marketing, product quality was a significant point of differentiation among product offerings. Some products delivered quality, others didn't. Astute consumers learned quickly which products to buy. Then, as quality universally improved, companies began to understand the potential value of differentiating themselves by creating a strong brand image. As a result, consumers not only looked for a quality product but also one whose brand image was most consistent with their own self-image.

According to studies by BBDO Worldwide, many products and services in today's "parity quality" categories have developed equally strong brand images. We believe that, in a marketplace characterized by strong brands and parity quality, consumers are open to new criteria to help them simplify their purchasing decisions. Customer focus (delivering delight) seems to be the most logical next point of differentiation. As providers of products and services successfully bond with their customers,

---

Management's Perspective

- Nurturing customer equity (the yin to brand equity's yang) can become a differentiating asset to competing organizations of the new economy.

- Customer equity will be developed through an accurate and unique understanding of one's customers' needs and by exceeding their expectations in one's operations, thereby creating delight.

these companies will begin to recognize the importance and value of their dedicated customers. They will begin to cultivate and value what we call "customer equity"—the value of dedicated and loyal customers.

Updating Our Marketing Strategies

One outcome of delivering delight in the new economy is that the role of marketing in an organization is bound to both change and expand. As the business function that is closest to the customer, marketing must champion the outside-in, service-oriented organization perspective. As it accomplishes this change in orientation, marketing must also modify its focus and scope.

Marketing as the Helmsman

Marketing's primary charge is to understand the wants, needs, and expectations of current and potential customers, feeding this information into the business organization to help it create and distribute products or services that more closely address and answer these inherent needs.

Marketing as the Customer Connection

A secondary but highly related role for marketing is to create and strengthen connections with customers. What is too often underappreciated is that there are several important ways to connect the customer to the organization. The most crucial ones are the customer-product connection, the customer service–delivery connection, and the customer-finances connection.

- The customer-product connection is the traditional domain of marketing. The "4 Ps" of price, promotion, product, and place (physical distribution) all connect the customer to the product.
- The customer service–delivery connection is the domain of customer satisfaction measurement and of continuous service improvement.
- The customer-finances connection relates customer satisfaction and customer behavior to profitability. This focus on return on service is a relatively recent addition to marketing management.

According to the *Journal of Marketing* article "The Role of Marketing," the value of the marketing function within an organization is positively related to how well marketing manages the customer-product and customer-finances connections; for service firms, that same value is positively related to how well marketing manages the customer service–delivery connection. Furthermore, the higher marketing is valued within the organization, the greater the financial outcomes.

Marketing as Learning Relationships

Too many companies long for relationships with their customers. The truth of the matter is, it's a one-sided longing. While some do (for instance, the strategic alliance formed in many business-to-business situations), most customers don't long to establish a relationship with a company. The root of the relationship goal is the marketer's perspective that, with a relationship, customers will be less likely to leave. This means that the underlying strategy is retention; establishing a relationship is merely a tactic to help accomplish that goal.

It's very important that we as companies recognize customers' general disregard for a relationship with us. The key to relationship formation is knowledge. The customer and the company in essence develop a learning relationship that provides value for both. For example, the longer we transact (relate) with the Internet search engine Yahoo!, the more Yahoo! learns about us and is subsequently better able to serve us. And the longer we transact with Yahoo!, the more difficult it will be to break our relationship because there is true value in our interactions with the search engine.

It is imperative that marketers look for ways to make relationships valuable to customers as well as to themselves. Many of us experience some value of relating with an airline, for instance, when we are shown recognition by being allowed to board early or are given the opportunity for an upgrade. Such an experience keeps customers coming back.

Marketing as Retention

The traditional textbook definition of marketing (which is arguably conquest-oriented) is giving way to an understanding that marketing is not only responsible for attracting the right customers but also for keeping them. While customer relationship management (CRM) is quickly becoming the buzzword of the 2000s, there is scant information on exactly how to manage relationships. Many computer-hardware manufacturers and most of the big-five consulting firms have established CRM practices, yet the most prominent results from these organizations are tactical: buy a bigger computer, acquire relationship management systems, conduct customer identification programs. Nurturing and truly managing relationships calls for new skills, systems, and perspectives that have yet to be created.

The implications are clear and profound. Not only must marketing expand its importance within the organization, it must also extend its scope to include tasks beyond the 4 Ps, such as managing the customer satisfaction measurement and service delivery improvement efforts, as well as managing the links between customer satisfaction and profitability. Other functions within the organization might manage those links, but the unintended result is inevitably an inside-out perspective, because marketing's unique customer focus gets lost.

A Return to Ethics

Traditionally, people talk about ethics from a religious or moral standpoint. That is, it is better to be ethical because that makes one a better person or helps one achieve an afterlife or gives one better karma. We argue

---

The Evolution of Marketing

Because of the outside-in perspective required to effectively compete in the new economy, the function of marketing will become more central to an organization's management. In turn, marketing must redefine its perspective to embrace the value of interactions with customers, offering greater benefits to customers by leveraging information gained through the relationship and by understanding how to strategically manage customer relationships.

that ethics will be resurgent in the new economy, regardless of whether people are more moral, more religious, or more decent. Ethics will make a comeback if only because it will be a rational response to a change in circumstances. In other words, our prediction that ethical behavior will be increasingly valued is based primarily on economic theory.

Ethics and Information

The information revolution fosters ethical behavior through its effect on available information. To understand this, consider a petty criminal (for example, a writer of bad checks) in a small town. Because information is widely shared, the bad-check writer will have a difficult time continuing to write bad checks because his checks will no longer be accepted. This effect means that individuals who stay in a small town are motivated to adopt a more ethical code of behavior. Conversely, the bad-check writer may tend to gravitate toward a big city or wander from town to town seeking situations where not so much information about him is available. In other words, a greater amount of information available promotes more ethical behavior.

The information revolution makes more information available in several ways. Communications links are more widespread than ever, through such technologies as the fax machine and the Internet. Consider the "hate" or "sucks" sites on the World Wide Web. These portals of information sharing give any customer who feels wronged by a company the opportunity to instantly spread their stories by "word of mouse" throughout the computerized world. Even though no remedy is received by the sender, he or she can feel somewhat placated because he or she has been able to vent to hundreds, thousands, perhaps millions of others on the Internet about the unfortunate interaction with a company. Computerization makes vast amounts of information available to almost everyone. These technologies make it more difficult to hide unethical behavior, forcing both individuals and companies to become more ethical.

Ethics and Long-Term Relationships

The attention to service that will result from the information revolution foreshadows an increase in the length of relationships, because an outside-in, customer-focused business sees its connections with customers as long-term relationships rather than one-time transactions. Being ethical pays off when the customer has a decision about whether or not to do business with a company again. The reason the fly-by-night business moves from place to place is that existing customers are unlikely to return. In fact, the longer the intended customer relationship, the more a company loses when a customer defects, and, thus, the more that is lost by unethical behavior. So the move toward long-term relationships implied by the rise of service also indicates a rise in corporate ethics and community responsibility.

Ethics in Internal Management

The same factors that drive corporations to become more ethical with their customers and the outside community will also cause corporations to treat their employees more ethically. This is not simply due to the increased communications and the increased amount of information that is stored but also because the high-growth environment, and the employee scarcity that it engenders, makes the company value long-term employment. If more is lost when an employee leaves, there is a greater penalty for the unethical corporate behavior that would cause an employee to leave.

Modernizing the Marketing Plan

Where the Conventional Marketing Plan Fails

The prevalent form of the marketing plan, in which a company catalogs the plans it has for its products, is rooted in the industrial era. In that era,

Information and Ethics

The need to become more intimate with one's customers—to better customize offerings to more closely meet idiosyncratic needs—will place a new burden on organizations to become more ethical in how they gather, maintain, and guard the information that they collect through their "learning relationships" with customers.

the business usually revolved around physical products and the goal was to distribute them. The key product-marketing decisions came to be known as the 4 Ps (product, promotion, price, and place or physical distribution). The marketing plan for all of the firm's products was based on decisions that were made with respect to the 4 Ps. This approach reflects an inside-out, transaction-focused view. It is inside-out because the analysis starts with the product, and it is transaction-focused because customer relationships are not central to any element of the plan.

Organizing the Marketing Plan Around Customers

The service-oriented future demands a marketing plan that is rooted in the realities of a service-focused economy. This new marketing plan, will revolve around customers rather than products. The parts of the plan will be customer segments or even individual high-value customers, and within each segment the decisions will fall into two major categories—initial customer attraction and customer retention. This structure will ultimately affect the way the marketing function is organized.

We have previously suggested a structure for the marketing function that divides the department into a marketing department for attracting customers and a customer department for retaining current customers (see Figure 6.2). The Promus Companies have done exactly that: they have divided their marketing function into a customer attraction unit, which concentrates on "4 Ps" types of decisions, and a customer retention unit, which concentrates on customer satisfaction, relationship building, and customer retention.

New Information Needs

With this new marketing plan come new information needs. Whereas in the existing marketing plan the information needs are largely product-focused (sales, product profitability, advertising effectiveness, distribution effectiveness, competitive positioning, and competitive product strategy), in the new marketing plan the information needs are largely customer-focused (customer retention rates, lifetime value of customers, "share-of-wallet," customer profitability, cross-buying, and customer satisfaction survey results). Customers are monitored even more closely than products, and customers—along with employees—are viewed as the most important long-term assets of the corporation.

Figure 6.2 *Proposed Reorganization of the Marketing Function*

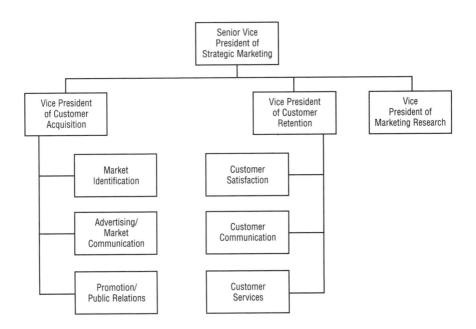

Summary

For either an individual wishing to have a successful career or a corporation wishing to survive the current radical economic changes, success in the new economy requires adopting a coherent approach that is consistent with the nature of the new economy.

The Rebirth of Loyalty

As a long-term view of customer relationships is adopted, loyalty becomes a very important concern. Loyalty is desired from both customers and employees. To earn loyalty, the company has to be willing to evince long-term commitment toward its most valuable employees. Similarly, through customer-retention programs the company must demonstrate a desire to form a long-term relationship with its high-value customers. The hoped-for results are attracting stable customers and employees who will become emotionally committed to the company rather than opportunistically switching from company to company. Again, this is a win-win situation

---

Marketing Tools of the New Economy

As marketing evolves to meet the challenges of the new economy, it will develop new metrics: customer lifetimes, lifetime values, customer satisfaction, customer loyalty, share of customer. These will replace the more traditional, macro measures of gross sales, gross margin, and share of market.

---

with both customers and employees gaining the sort of respect and commitment they desire in exchange for some commitment from them.

Why Service = Delight = Success

All of these transformations and developments indicate that delight-provoking service is the key to success. That is not said as a feel-good catchphrase but rather as the inevitable, rational result from a shift in the fundamental nature of the economy. Companies must serve customers better if they want to retain them for the long-term relationships that form the basis of the companies' economic success. And companies need to treat their employees better in order to retain them longer and to encourage them to give the better service that customers are seeking. Certainly both of these goals are compatible, even synergistic. Likewise, employees must identify to an even greater degree with the companies at which they work to permit the necessary long-term relationships to grow and flourish. In sum this spells the restoration of the traditional social contract between the company and the employee, in which a loyal employee is rewarded with money and security by the company. It also implies a closer, friendlier, more supportive relationship between the company and the customer.

The Optimists Are Right

Seen as a coherent pattern, it is apparent that the new economy is not just wishful thinking. Just like the Industrial Revolution a century before, the productivity gains finally achieved in the sector of transformation (in this case the service sector) permit a higher level of sustained growth. This growth level is bound to lead to an exciting era of economic expansion.

In addition, because the growth this time around is in information and service, those elements will also shape management in the new economy. The combination of growth, information, and service will inevitably lead to an unprecedented service-oriented, customer-oriented, and relationship-oriented economic future. For management, the future is excellent service in all of its ramifications and delighted customers.

Chapter Key Notes

- The new economy challenges businesses to leverage their interactions with their customers for two purposes:

  1. Building stronger relationships with customers
  2. Developing products and services to bond customers into a more dedicated commitment.

- Investing in customer loyalty develops for the firm the most valuable asset it can achieve: a dedicated, loyal, proselytizing customer base. The net value of such a group of committed customers is what we have labeled "customer equity."

Voices of Experience

IN MAY OF 1804, Lewis and Clark headed west along the Missouri River with the goal of reaching the Pacific Ocean. The mission had been secretly organized by President Thomas Jefferson and covertly approved by Congress, as it meant venturing beyond the territory of the young United States into land claimed by the British crown. Jefferson hoped that Lewis and Clark would find a water route to the Pacific to allow trade and emigration.

On December 5, 1805, Lewis and Clark reached the Pacific. In writing of their success, William Clark wrote, "We now discover that we have found the most practicable and navigable passage across the continent of North America." Clark, like so many explorers, was prematurely enthusiastic.

While Lewis and Clark proved that travel across the North American continent was possible, their route was far too difficult for wagons to travel. Lolo Pass, where their expedition crossed the Rocky Mountains, is difficult even today. Until a more hospitable route could be found, large-scale travel to the West would be impossible.

Seven years later, in 1812, Robert Stuart made an incredible discovery—a twenty-mile-wide gap in the Rocky Mountains where wagons could get through. Named South Pass, this passageway represented the true gateway through the Continental Divide. But John Jacob Astor, Stuart's employer, considered this information proprietary and to be of great value to his Pacific Fur Company. Astor successfully suppressed word of its existence.

Jedediah Smith, perhaps the greatest of all mountain men and one of America's greatest explorers, rediscovered South Pass in 1825, twelve years after Stuart. But this time Smith made certain that everyone knew of its existence—he even left behind a map. The so-called Fremont, Gibbs, Smith map would be the only accurate and comprehensive map of the American West for decades.

The discovery and communication of South Pass greatly influenced the history of the United States. Without it, wagon travel across the North American continent would not have been possible. As a result, Oregon and California probably would not have become a part of the United States. With this valuable information, however, more than half a million people would eventually flow through South Pass, and the United States would ultimately extend from the Atlantic to the Pacific.

The Gap Between Desire and Reality

Like Sara Lee, "Nobody doesn't want satisfied customers," and most managers would agree it would be beneficial to their businesses to have delighted customers. The enormous amounts of money currently being spent on customer relationship management (CRM) initiatives are evidence of this belief of the business community in general. But most managers also recognize that few firms consistently deliver customer delight—and it's likely, they would admit, that *their* firm is not among those select few that do. It is as if a great Delight Divide exists between a firm's ability to create mere satisfaction and its goal of consistently creating delight.

Unfortunately, the path to customer delight comes with few guideposts and no universal map. To compound the difficulty, all too frequently managers misinterpret the information they get from customers, which causes them to focus on issues that have little impact on delight, much the same way Lewis and Clark valued their impractical passage.

The early chapters of this book discussed the issues involved in correctly collecting and interpreting customer delight information. We have established that, without a complete understanding of the shape of the relationship between satisfaction and behavior (the Delight Progression), it is virtually impossible to correctly prioritize the most promising opportunities for improvement. The resulting misallocation has had unfortunate and costly consequences, frequently resulting in a disjunction between satisfaction levels and business results.

While the correct prioritization of improvement opportunities is vitally important to successfully implementing a customer delight strategy, this information alone does not guarantee success. Assuming that managers have correctly identified where to focus their efforts, a host of other issues impact how to do it. It is one thing to have an accurate map, quite another to have a road-worthy vehicle to get you to your destination.

The Business Context

The business situation within which a firm competes has an enormous effect on the results a delight initiative is likely to generate. Following is a discussion of three of the most influential:

1. The nature of competition and the industry. Except for an occasional new start-up, most companies today compete in very aggressive categories in which competition is extremely hungry. These industries are also mature so strategic positionings are spoken for; the situation, while aggressive, is nevertheless reasonably stable. In such situations customer delight can be an attractive, competitive strategy. The companies featured in our case studies compete in very aggressive categories (see Chapters 8, 9, and 10).

2. The uniqueness of the product or service. Most companies today lack a well-differentiated or unique product or service. One company offers essentially what everyone else offers. Our markets have become populated by parity quality—products and services are no better nor worse than the competition's. In such situations, customers look for other cues to help them distinguish one provider from another. It is our belief that customer delight can become a substantial differentiator.

3. Organizational rigidity. The openness of the firm to change can also substantially affect the outcome of a delight initiative. In order for the delight program to succeed, two needs must be met: visibility and support from the company. In situations in which the corporate structure is both revered and openly opposed to change, those needs are less likely to be met than in situations in which the structure is open to change. The battle cry to organize around the customer can have rather severe implications for a very rigid, traditional corporate organization.

Delight initiatives can be assigned to existing departments' functions. In this respect a customer service, marketing, marketing research, or sales department might be asked to oversee and operate the new program. In contrast, programs for which an entire department and its responsibilities are created demonstrate much more of a commitment—a key to success—than those in which supporting activities are simply "borrowed" or redirected.

The Design Process

Gaining the insights necessary to strategically focus on elements of delight requires an intimate view of the business process that a firm is involved in, the exact nature of one's customers, and those customers' need states. Few managers have such insights readily at hand. Instead, a discovery process will need to be launched to help identify all of the peculiarities of the situation.

Precipitating Conditions

To most fully appreciate the success of a customer delight initiative, it is valuable to understand just how the commitment to achieve maximum customer delight was initially made. Oftentimes, *proactive*, innovative programs are created out of the insight that striving for customer delight is the best and most appropriate strategy for competing in one's category. Programs that are *reactive* are more likely to be copycat versions of a competitor's unique innovation. When looking at the history of a firm's delight initiatives consider this question: Was the program the pioneering effort in the category or was it merely a catch-up, parity-maintaining effort? The innovative firm will probably be more invested in the delight-initiative effort.

Corporate Sponsorship

Who championed the delight initiative? We've seen very few top-driven programs fail. Even if they're not the best-designed program, they'll be made to work because everyone in the organization clearly understands that this is what top management desires. On the other hand, programs championed by impassioned individuals from midmanagement ranks are less likely to succeed. Some excellently designed programs have failed because midlevel management simply didn't possess the resources, authority, and clout necessary to lead a persuasive campaign for its adoption.

Program Design

Another important aspect of the delight initiative is the origination of the form and content. Intuitively designed programs that sound reasonable though have no research to back them up, while arguably better than none at all, will be less effective than a correctly designed program. Proper design involves soliciting input and coordinating the varied ideas from a disparate group of sources. These include, but need not be limited to:

- Current management
- Line workers (employees with direct customer contact)
- Current customers
- Past customers
- Customers of competitors; reactions to programs offered by competitors in the category
- Organizations with world-class programs, not necessarily in one's own industry
- Industry experts or critics
- Customer service and satisfaction professionals

Expectations

Programs should have clearly defined goals and deliverables. Delight programs, unlike so many other elements of marketing, can be held accountable for results. With appropriate baseline measures, the improvements gained by the program can be monitored over time. Specific performance goals should also be linked to a realistic timetable. Everyone should understand the measures to be used and the timetable and should be encouraged to share in the ownership of the results.

Learning from the Best

While there is no one right path to implementing a customer delight strategy, a number of common themes exist among successful firms. In the following chapters you will read stories of three very different firms that have embarked on a customer delight strategy.

Chapter 8 presents the case of Roche Diagnostic Systems, maker of diagnostic instrumentation and test reagents for use by clinical- and drug abuse–testing professionals. The case study presents the issues facing a new president who has the opportunity to transform a division that had rarely met its profit objectives since its inception. Customer delight was the chosen strategy; the results are quite incredible—profitability in just three short years, world-class stature within six to eight.

Chapter 9 presents the case of Toys "R" Us, the largest retailer of toys and children's products in the world. The case of Toys "R" Us highlights the challenges faced by the company in the wake of increasing competition and eroding market share where delight was momentarily forgotten. Toys "R" Us revitalized its commitment to measure and thereby improve its customers' shopping experiences.

Chapter 10 presents the case of Mercedes-Benz USA, a wholly owned subsidiary of DaimlerChrysler AG. Mercedes-Benz is unique in its cultural devotion to its customers and its organization around the customer. The company has built an internal department that is responsible for all owner contact. This department, the Client Assistance Center, unites five areas of on-going interaction with the company's customers. We believe this organizational structure sets a standard for all organizations that wish to strategically engineer and monitor the delight of their customers.

These firms come from a variety of industries and starting points. Each is at a different point in their journey, but they all have developed a clear and well-reasoned plan for consistently delighting their customers. Their struggles and successes provide a guide through the Delight Divide.

Summary

To make the following case studies of maximum value to you, try reviewing in light of the criteria we've discussed. Specifically:

• What was each company's business environment? What was their industry's position in its life cycle? What was the nature of their competition? What were the conditions for growth in their category?

• What was the company's competitive position prior to committing to customer delight? Was the commitment reactive (born out of despair) or proactive (a continuing effort of their strategic management initiatives)?

- What role did the sponsoring company play in its industry? That of visionary or that of follower?

- What was the company's immediate history, specifically with regard to interacting with its customers?

- Was customer satisfaction already on the company's "corporate instrument panel" or did the delight initiative place it there?

- What departments and which individuals led the drive? Was it top-driven or did middle management champion the initiative?

- How were the costs of customer delight accepted? Were monitoring processes established to help ascertain payback from delight?

- Did the organizational infrastructure already exist, or was a new department and executive empowered to conduct the program?

- How was the vision created? How, if at all, was benchmarking used? What was the role of customers in the design? What was the role of company management?

- What sort of financial rewards were related to the success of the program? How pervasive (dispersed throughout the organization) were they?

- What time frame was established for setting up the program and for observing the first results?

The Case of Roche Diagnostic Systems

Parts of this case were included in the article "Customer Delight and the Bottom Line" by Timothy L. Keiningham, Melinda K. M. Goddard, Terry G. Vavra, and Andrew J. Iaci, which appeared in the Fall 1999 issue of Marketing Management.

IN APRIL 1991 Carlo Medici, general manager of the Italian affiliate of Roche Diagnostic Systems, found himself confronted with a life-altering decision. At the time, Medici was riding high. The Italian affiliate he headed had amassed tremendous success. Sales were approaching that of its U.S. counterpart, which by any measure should have been five to six times greater.

As would be expected, this success did not go unnoticed. Jean-Luc Bélingard, chairman of the global division, hoped that Medici could make a similar transformation for the U.S. affiliate. Bélingard approached Medici with an offer to become the president of Roche Diagnostic Systems in the United States.

Roche Diagnostic Systems began as a small, yet global division of F. Hoffmann-La Roche Ltd. in 1969, with headquarters in Switzerland and with its largest affiliates in the United States, Italy, France, and Japan. The business centered on diagnostic instrumentation and test reagents for use by clinical- and drug abuse–testing professionals. By 1990 the lines included blood cultures, chemistry (and later, hematology) instruments, drug abuse–testing kits, pregnancy tests, and tumor-monitoring assays.

Roche Diagnostics pursued a product-driven strategy, focusing on innovation as its key source of differentiation. Unfortunately, Medici notes, the "product portfolio was not in synch with the market—an aging product, fast approaching the end of the life cycle with no replacement whatsoever being planned, and a huge gap in terms of development plans for the future generation of products." Furthermore, while all of the products could intellectually be thought of as being within the same market, they actually addressed the needs of very different customer segments. The result was that the U.S. affiliate of Roche Diagnostic Systems was rarely a primary vendor or partner to customers in any one segment, except for drug abuse–testing in U.S. criminal justice, drug treatment, and workplace testing sectors. Not surprisingly, the affiliate seldom achieved its profit objectives subsequent to its founding in 1969.

The Challenge of Improvement

Despite the problems the U.S. arm was experiencing, Medici looked upon the opportunity with enthusiasm. He became president of the U.S. division in January 1992. When he arrived at the division's headquarters, however, the situation was worse than he had expected. "I found a situation with a stagnant product portfolio, no creative marketing, a very dormant sales organization, a very broken management team, combined with an overall division that was struggling in terms of finding its way in the future," recalls Medici. "That was a recipe for disaster."

Medici quickly went to work establishing his vision for Roche Diagnostic Systems. He put together a five-year strategic plan, naming it the Challenge to Change. The vision for that plan was that Roche Diagnostics would achieve leadership and profitability through customer delight. "I felt at the time that the [product] portfolio could not help me 100 percent," notes Medici. "I said, 'I will not bitch and moan with the headquarters because I am part of the process of revamping the portfolio.'"

But consistently poor results and the known weaknesses in the product portfolio had taken its toll on the morale of the company. "I needed to give these people a reason to hope for the future while we were fixing the portfolio," explains Medici. "I truly believed that the customer satisfaction piece, putting the focus on the customer and really managing all parts of the organization with the demand side—macro and micro—was the best way to do it."

The launching of Challenge to Change represented a tectonic shift for the organization. In management meetings, Medici explained that the company would rigorously pursue the measurement and management of customer satisfaction. Furthermore, the focus would not be on simply satisfying the customer; the customer must be delighted.

Unfortunately, Medici discovered that credibility was very low and that most believed his program was simply a fad that would blow over in a few months. He still recalls with amazement the reactions he received to the plan:

> I remember somebody asked me a question. I still remember his name— John. John asked me, "Carlo, are you going to share the results of the survey with us?" I walked toward him thinking to myself, "Why am I here—I want my mama." It was then I realized that not only do they not believe [in the program] and think I'm crazy, but that before this they were never part of any solution. They were never told how bad the situation was.

Medici's response to the question was a jaw dropper for the company: "Why would we do a survey and not share the results with you? But actually, there is much more. You are going to be in charge of fixing whatever issues are discovered from the survey."

Establishing Measures

Upon launching Challenge to Change, the U.S. organization began a systematic approach to customer satisfaction measurement and initiatives. The first step was a qualitative, exploratory phase consisting of focus groups with customers. The groups were employed to gain an understanding of the critical interactions between Roche Diagnostic Systems and its customers from which customers form their opinions of the company's level of service. Such interactions are frequently referred to as moments of truth because they represent implicit promises by the company to the customer.

The company then turned to the frontline employees to compare and confirm their findings. Focus groups were conducted with sales representatives, instrument repair and service engineers, on-site technical specialists, the home-office training staff, telephone technical specialists, customer-service representatives, and account services and credit specialists. In short, everyone who had direct customer contact and responsibility was involved in this process.

From the customer's perspective, the business relationship began (and ended) with the decision to purchase and/or to tell colleagues to do the same. The customer interacted with the Roche business development representative to support his or her buying decision, followed by working with the Roche team responsible for the installation of the new analytic system. The customer company's staff then traveled to the Roche home office for training. They were then accompanied back to their laboratory by the Roche installation team, which would ensure that the clinical system was validated according to established quality control and performance standards to reliably report patient results. To access support, the customer called a toll-free number for ordering and account-services assistance, for first-line technical assistance, and, if needed, to dispatch on-site technical or repair specialists who would assist them throughout a typical instrument life cycle of five to seven years. Every moment of truth would then shape the customer's opinion of the company, as well as his or her personal referrals, which represented a vital aspect of this highly specialized capital equipment market.

The moments of truth established in the qualitative phase were then used as the underlying structure for the development of a customer satisfaction questionnaire. As it was not possible to know from the qualitative research the degree of influence each moment of truth had on a customer's level of satisfaction, the original survey included more than seventy-five aspects of these identified processes.

Once the questionnaire structure was determined, an appropriate response scale needed to be selected. A frequent problem with satisfaction response scales is the skewed distribution they produce, with an inordinate number of responses at the most favorable end of the scale. To combat this effect, Roche decided to use a scale weighted, or biased, to the lower, unsatisfactory extreme. The rationale was that this scale would give customers ample opportunity to rate the company as realistically as possible. The scale selected was a 5-point, negatively biased Likert scale: Very Satisfied, Satisfied, Somewhat Dissatisfied, Dissatisfied, and Very Dissatisfied. (From a communication perspective, this scale could be accused of planting the notion that Roche wasn't very satisfactory. In the current situation, however, Medici braved the consequences, knowing that the condition of the company was dire.)

The last design issue to be considered was the appropriate means of administering the survey. Because of issues of timeliness and the need to be able to interactively probe customers for explanations of some answers, telephone interviewing was selected for conducting the survey. The length of the survey, however, required setting appointments, especially with physicians, and offering honoraria to keep these professionals—typically extremely busy—on the phone long enough (about an hour) to complete the survey.

Establishing Benchmarks and Setting Goals

By the fourth quarter of 1992, the initial interviews were completed and included 508 customers across the various lines of the business. At first glance, the results did not appear condemningly poor. While 36 percent of customers expressed that they were Very Satisfied (the top level of satisfaction), 15 percent described themselves as Somewhat to Very Dissatisfied overall. Similar 5-point Likert-scale surveys showed that 39 percent would Definitely Buy Again, while 57 percent would Definitely Recommend the company's products.

In response to these results, the internal question became, "How do we use this information to improve our processes?" The problem is that for satisfaction information to provide a clear mandate for change, it must be comparable against some benchmark, either the performance of a competitor or performance goals previously established by management. It must also in some way be linked to the business processes that are managed and monitored on a day-to-day basis within a company.

To gain the perspective needed to understand both satisfaction and process measurements, the company participated in an industry-wide audit of global healthcare industry manufacturers that was conducted by Coopers and Lybrand. The audit analyzed hundreds of internal metrics and established the industry-relative ranking in each aspect of service.

These metrics corresponded well with the moments of truth measured in the customer satisfaction surveys for Roche. As with the satisfaction surveys, the process metrics included numerous factors, such as the speed of arrival for engineers and technical representatives, the response speed of the hot line, the "first-time-fix rate" for the hot line and the field staff, and dozens more. These metrics were then matched to the survey dimensions (based on prima facie validity) to construct a sort of parallel universe in which the customers' perspectives could be analyzed from an operational level for each process affecting the service levels the customers experienced. Approximately seventy metrics were selected for routine review, with each process owner established as an owner of a portion of the metrics. It was the duty of the process owner to compare the industry performance on each of these aspects with the relative satisfaction score collected from Roche customers. There were many metrics on which Roche fell short of industry practice and on which Roche customers gave particularly low satisfaction ratings. Performance goals were then set based on these concurrences.

One of the earliest satisfaction-survey challenges came when various departments realized their procedures needed to improve if they wanted to achieve higher levels of efficiency and customer satisfaction. In defense, the water cooler question became, "Aren't all customers hard to please?" followed by the reassuring refrain that "maybe we aren't so bad after all." To answer these concerns, a survey was conducted of customers from competitive, best-in-class companies in order to compare competitors' results with the Roche satisfaction results. Sixty percent of the leading companies' customers reported that they were Very Satisfied overall; only 8 percent expressed any level of dissatisfaction. This was approximately half the level of dissatisfaction expressed by Roche customers.

Preparing Roche for Change

In 1993 the combination of relatively low rankings in critical performance measures—customer delight and overall market share and revenues—culminated in Medici's decision to form a Benchmarking Task Force that included the Roche key stakeholders in each major service-quality process. In the beginning, however, such meetings did not always go smoothly. In one of the first Steering Committee meetings, Medici discovered first-hand that the company had not yet embraced the strategy of customer delight—he found himself sitting in a virtually empty room. Fifteen minutes after the meeting was scheduled to start, only two out of twelve people had showed up. Medici recalls:

> I just left the meeting and I slammed the door. I sent an E-mail to the [no-shows] that quite frankly had some people ready to resign. I basically said, "You obviously don't give a damn about customer satisfaction and you just do it

because I told you to do so. This is not what I expect of a management team that is engaged and committed. So if you are not committed, just please tell me now. Come see me and I'll help you. But if you are committed, truly committed, this will not happen again. You will be on time. You will show up. You will be prepared. And you will be committed. I won't accept any excuse. There is nothing more important than meeting the demands of our customers and deciding what to do to improve our level of satisfaction with this company!"

If there was any uncertainty about Medici's commitment and passion, this left no doubt. And this situation never occurred again.

Medici's passion, however, came with a price. Turnover in the management ranks was high. In the course of Medici's career at the U.S. arm of Roche Diagnostics, the management team was turned over almost 100 percent. According to Medici, "People were fired, people were hired, people were promoted, and people were counseled to go somewhere else." Noting that not every person has the desire or ability to serve customers, he says, "You want to help them, and in the end you help people go where they will be better off."

First Steps

The Benchmarking Task Force pored over the results of the customer satisfaction survey. Every facet of customer support was analyzed. Improvements were pursued, solutions proposed, and implementation approved based on three main considerations:

1. Gap analysis ("Worst first")

2. Quick hits ("Low-hanging fruit")

3. Available resources, given a highly volatile financial scenario

Meanwhile, first steps to increase profits were being taken.

One of the trouble spots that Roche identified early on concerned the diagnostic system repair process. While the repair process was meeting internal requirements, it was not delighting customers. "We realized that first our service engineers, the ones who repair the machines, ought to 'repair' the customer more than the machine. And second, they ought to do more than what they were doing at the time," explains Medici.

One problem was that repairing the mechanical breakdown did not necessarily mean that the customer could immediately use the diagnostic system. Instead, the instrument had to be reprogrammed and that required some components that the engineers were not trained to handle. Adding to the difficulty, their manager had specifically told them, "This is not your job."

The decision was made to change the approach. The service engineers would be trained in communications skills so that they could relate to the doctor responsible for the office and the technician responsible for the diagnostic system. The engineers would also be cross-trained to program the instrument, working in tandem with technical specialists at Roche.

This change represented a tremendous shift in the way things were done at Roche and it was not universally welcome. Medici says, "I remember being in a sales meeting when we announced this program and our intention. I knew that there were some engineers—I knew them by name—who would not accept this. They were part of the old school."

As Medici entered the sales meeting to make his presentation, he observed that these people were grouped together speaking with one another. Discussing his proposed changes, he approached them. Speaking to the group Medici said, "I want to make it very clear this is the direction we are taking. I realize that some of you may not be comfortable with it. We'll help you any way we can. If you feel that this is not the right direction, we respect your decision, but this is where we're going and I need 100 percent commitment."

Over the course of the next ninety days, about one-third of the engineers resigned. This presented serious challenges to Roche Diagnostics in the short term, but over time, customer delight with engineering support improved significantly. "You have to be ready to take a hard stance and accept some issues in the short term," observes Medici. "But you hire the right caliber of people who are committed to cross-train, who are committed to 'fixing' the customer and the machine."

Amplifying the Voice of the Customer

With each improvement, the established customer survey provided continuous feedback on key initiatives and helped maintain the customer focus in the organization at a national level. For the first two years, the survey results were analyzed in relatively conventional ways, being limited to aggregate statistics and simple listings of the verbatim responses to the open-ended questions in the survey. This aggregated data prompted a rather predictable process of rationalization among the departments or regions. Wherever suboptimal processes were shared, it was too easy for one department or region to focus on another with an equally poor or poorer performance. More specific analyses were needed to build stronger feelings of process ownership.

In 1994 Melinda Goddard joined Medici's task force as the manager of customer satisfaction. Goddard was convinced more information could be derived from the customer surveying that was being conducted (mostly internally). She transferred the data analysis to an external marketing consulting firm. This firm practiced multivariate analyses and also had a unique expertise in manipulating and processing responses to open-ended questions. One of the first improvements Goddard implemented was the ordering of attributes by their linkage with key criteria variables. This process, called *key-driver analysis*, helped the regions and departments focus more accutely on improving those practices that really mattered. Drill-downs, whereby explanatory verbatims were associated with certain levels of dissatisfaction on the most important attributes, were also provided. This new in-depth analysis enabled Roche to provide a high degree of specificity in process feedback at both the regional and the departmental levels.

The explanatory verbatims brought the voice of the customer directly to the responsible employees and gave them feedback about the weaknesses of their processes, something none of the financial statements could do. Furthermore, key-word searching of verbatim responses to the more general questions in the survey enabled the company to eliminate dozens of more specific questions from the survey. This streamlining allowed customers to be surveyed in a concise, fifteen-minute interview. Another benefit was the elimination of appointment scheduling, as most of the Roche customers were willing to speak for fifteen to twenty minutes upon first contact without requiring a scheduling call and without expecting an honorarium (due in large part to their relative investment in and dependence upon their Roche system in performing their work).

The key-driver analyses were used to demonstrate definitive relationships between customer delight, repurchase intentions, referral intentions, and root causes. This information reinforced the compelling business case that proved to all employees the importance of striving for top-category satisfaction. It was dramatically evident that merely satisfied customers were far less likely to buy again or give referrals to their colleagues than their delighted counterparts.

A Process-Improvement Example

As departments or regions implemented and completed database-driven customer delight initiatives, the key-driver analysis also helped answer the question, What do we work on next? One tool used to assist in the identification of the best opportunities for improvement and communicating their importance was the performance-importance grid, or quadrant chart (see Figure 8.1). In this chart the importance of a moment of truth (in this case, as measured by its correlation to overall delight) was plotted versus the percent of customers who rated themselves as delighted with Roche on this area.

Figure 8.1 *Performance-Importance Grid*

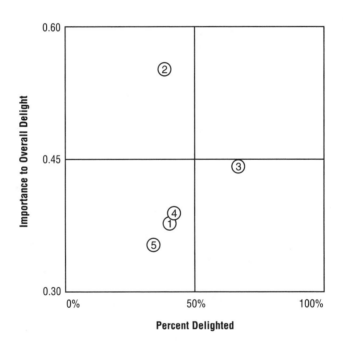

1) Training

2) Phone Support

3) Instrument Support

4) On-site Tech Support

5) Orders/Deliveries

This quadrant chart shows that the toll-free telephone support represented an opportunity for improvement since it was of relatively high importance and yet, at the time, was relatively low in delight performance. While the importance of telephone support was intuitively understood, the causes of customer dissatisfaction required more investigation.

When customers called into Roche Diagnostic Systems in the United States, they were immediately "greeted" by an automated voice response system and given prompts to select either technical assistance, ordering assistance, paging for a service engineer, or product information. Selecting "technical assistance" resulted in a second set of prompts to determine the product category. After selecting the product category customers were then forwarded to one of six dedicated technical-service operators who only took messages. These messages were then put into a computerized queuing system for medical technologists, who were then to call customers back. None of these calls were transferred live to a medical technologist. (Internally, Roche measured the quality of its technical assistance with a metric called Time to Call Back, which measured how long it took to call a customer back.)

Customers who selected "ordering assistance" were sent to one of fourteen customer-service representatives. If a customer had a question about a product, however, that resulted in a transfer to one of the technical-service operators. Likewise, when speaking to a technical-service operator, if a customer had an ordering question, the customer was transferred to a customer-service representative. In any given month, between 20 percent and 40 percent of calls required transfers between operators and customer-service representatives.

If customers selected "paging for an engineer," they were immediately transferred to a technical-service operator who then paged an engineer through a remote paging system—regardless of the situation. The field engineer would then interrupt a service call or wait for the next phone booth on the road to call the customer back from the field.

Those customers requesting "product information" never got the opportunity to speak with anyone. They were simply transferred into a message mailbox for a follow-up mailing.

Looking at the telephone support process, it quickly became apparent that, like many processes within companies, it had evolved incrementally and was put together piecemeal, tying different Roche functional areas together. The result was an internal approach to customer communication, not an external, customer focus. Evidence of this can be readily seen in internal metrics like "Time to Call Back" (used to measure technical assistance). While the measure was true to the process, customers did not want to be called back. They wanted immediate, live access to assistance. In terms of improving customer satisfaction, it was a useless metric.

It was obvious that a customer-focused solution required instituting a change in process. It was decided that customers' questions should be answered in a timely manner, with personal interaction, and with as few transfers as possible. To eliminate the 20 percent to 40 percent of calls transferred between departments, Roche created one group of operators consisting of customer-service representatives who were cross-trained to provide ordering assistance when needed, give basic product information, and transfer calls to the medical technologists for further product and technical-service information. A customer requesting product information would be transferred to a mailing queue; however, they were given the opportunity to speak with a medical technologist if they could not wait for product literature to be mailed. To streamline the process even more, the medical technologists were grouped into product teams, allowing customer-service representatives to make live transfers to a specific team whenever highly detailed assistance was required. The medical technologists could then page an engineer to see if he or she could help them fix the problem over the telephone without the customer having to wait for the engineer to call back. Also, field engineers worked at the call center on a rotating basis to assist with telephone support throughout the day. These changes had the added benefit of centralizing knowledge about specific problems.

The result of this improvement effort was an end to the automated voice response system during normal business hours. More importantly, it resulted in a significant increase in the number of customers who were Very Satisfied with Roche telephone support. Likewise, there was an increase in the number of customers who were Very Satisfied with Roche Diagnostic Systems overall (see Figure 8.2).

It is important to note that increases in overall satisfaction are likely to be a function of increases in satisfaction with the improvement efforts, including telephone support, that occurred simultaneously. Because of the strength of the relationship, however, it is clear that improvements in telephone support played a significant role in the improvement of overall satisfaction with Roche Diagnostic Systems in the United States.

Figure 8.2 *Percent Delighted with Telephone Support Compared to Percent Delighted Overall*

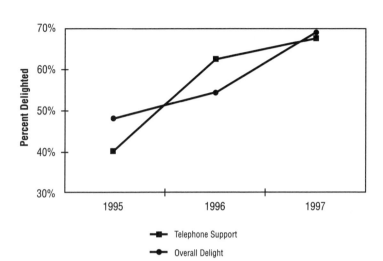

Did It Pay Off?

When Roche Diagnostic Systems began its customer delight focus, most customers would have rated themselves as satisfied with the service they received from Roche. The division's new management quickly learned, however, that having satisfied customers was not generating expected profits. The management realized that satisfaction was not enough—customers had to be delighted with Roche for the division to succeed.

All of the efforts to move customers beyond mere satisfaction, however, would have been for naught if they were not demonstrably linked to division profitability. When Medici presented the Challenge to Change, it was a five-year strategic plan. Under the plan, Roche Diagnostics would not break even until 1995—three years after Medici took over as president. And there were a number of assumptions in the plan, including that the company would have a different product portfolio in 1996 than it did in 1992. According to Medici:

> Without the portfolio changes, [success] would not have happened. Customer delight is a winning strategy, but it needs to be accompanied with your value proposition. . . . We needed to fix the product, the quality of services, and the customer satisfaction piece, which are intertwined—actually inseparable.

Roche, however, had carefully prioritized its improvement efforts. It focused improvement initiatives on the most important issues (as identified by the key-driver analyses). Consequently its proportion of delighted customers grew, and so did its sales and profits (see Figure 8.3).

Roche Diagnostic Systems went from a low growth division into the fastest-growing competitor in its industry and in the F. Hoffmann-La Roche Ltd. worldwide healthcare group. Medici states proudly:

> We grew ten times the market average. [By 1997 there was a] management team committed to customer delight, so that we're not just selling good products, we're really nurturing the customer relationship and really focusing on all the aspects of customer delight. When you have a business with 98 percent to 99 percent repurchase intention and zero dissatisfaction, boy, it looks good! You feel like you closed the cycle. You achieved the Challenge to Change.

Summary

The U.S. affiliate of Roche Diagnostic Systems was not achieving its profit objectives when Carlo Medici was named president in 1992. Because new products alone would not solve the company's problems (and new products would not be available for some time), Medici decided to focus on improving the level of customer satisfaction with the company.

Figure 8.3 *Overall Satisfaction Compared to Roche Diagnostic Systems Profitability*

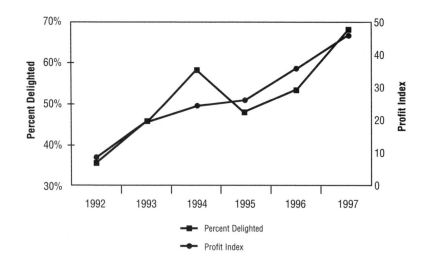

Medici realized that it was imperative to overcome the slow and reluctant buy-in that improvement efforts traditionally receive. Roche Diagnostics teamed numerical analysis with processes for mining verbal responses of customers. While the numerical results established priorities for improvement, the verbal responses served as convincing arguments to line personnel, exposing how important their performance was to customer satisfaction.

Furthermore, Medici consistently demonstrated his commitment to customer delight and demanded that commitment from everyone in the organization. He was willing to accept the short-term pain associated with implementing his plan for having a team totally committed to customer delight.

In short, dedicated process management and insightful executive guidance harnessed the information discovered through customer satisfaction surveys and used this information to successfully transform Roche Diagnostic Systems through the customer delight principle.

The Case of Toys "R" Us

The authors thank Susan Boche, director of customer relations at Toys "R" Us, for joining them in discussing the difficulties of attaining customer delight.

TOYS "R" US IS the largest retailer of toys and children's products in the world, with total annual revenues of more than $11 billion. From a single toy store opened in 1957, the company now operates more than 700 Toys "R" Us stores in the United States and more than 450 international stores in twenty-seven countries. In recognition of its tremendous success, in March 2000 Toys "R" Us was honored with the Lebhar-Friedman "Best of the Century" award for hard-line retailers.

The success of Toys "R" Us, however, made it the target of numerous competitors. Specialty stores have sought to take away sales, as have two noncategory giants, Wal-Mart and Target. As a result, throughout the nineties the company has watched its share of the toy market decline.

In an effort to curb the erosion in its market share, Toys "R" Us began changing the layout of its stores to make them more attractive and easier to shop. Without question, the company needed to change its store format. Customers found that the no-frills structure, a cornerstone of its early success, now seemed dated. Too often store designs were drab, toys were stocked floor to ceiling, and lighting was dim.

But Toys "R" Us had developed a problem that went beyond its store design—the company had developed a well-publicized reputation for poor service.

- "Now the formula no longer works and the shareholders are getting poorer. Toys 'R' Us is no longer the cheapest store in town, although its service remains awful." —Paul Klebnikov, *Forbes*, 1998

- "The top brass at Toys 'R' Us would only need to make an occasional visit to the customer service department at any of their major outlets to see that the system was no longer working. . . . The public understands that at category killers you're not going to get the kind of hand-holding you might get at a Mercedes-Benz dealership. But you don't expect to be treated like an insolent galley slave either." —Joe Queenan, *Chief Executive*, 1998

- "Faced with this, Toys 'R' Us still clings to its old format. . . . As for the service: It stinks." —Katrina Brooker, *Fortune*, 1999

New Game, New Rules

While the reputation for poor service may not have been unfounded, Toys "R" Us did not ignore service. In fact, quite the opposite was true. Throughout the 1990s Toys "R" Us was spending millions of dollars each year to both measure and improve customers' shopping experience. Achieving customer satisfaction and service thresholds were also a key component of store managers' compensation.

Year after year, however, research was showing no improvement in customers' perceptions of their overall shopping experience. At this point the internal information systems at Toys "R" Us became a focal point for management to understand what the company's strengths and weaknesses were in the context of the attack being waged by its competitors. Susan Boche, newly appointed director of customer relations, was asked to try to get a handle on the dynamics of the situation.

The increasing frustration with consistently seeing flat-line results for their efforts created an understandable focus within Toys "R" Us to "move the line." Annoyed at being unable to move the line, Boche reacted flippantly one day when examining the results. She simply changed the scale on her graphs, which magnified tiny differences between points on the graph. For her, this was an epiphany. "Moving the line translated into changing the numbers, which translated into what had become a company-wide focus-on-numbers," recalls Boche. Moving the numbers, however, did not translate into understanding what customers meant by their ratings. As a result, the numbers didn't translate into changes in service in the stores that were meaningful to customers.

As she took an inventory of the situation, it was obvious to Boche that the satisfaction-monitoring system she had inherited was frustrating management at stores across the country. Boche explains:

> Everybody was trying really hard to make positive changes. Everybody thought they knew what we needed to do but no improvement occurred as a result! At the time we had a great deal of information. We were conducting mystery shops, a satisfaction-tracking study, and a national study of competition in the industry. None of the studies seemed to have any relationship with one another. Not only didn't the numbers correlate with one another, they also failed to correlate with any actions taken in the stores.

Random Luck

Toys "R" Us store managers felt they were being evaluated by a system that was totally out of touch with reality. Sometimes the numbers would be numerically down with no identifiable cause; other times the numbers would be numerically up, even though the manager had done nothing to improve the shopping experience in the store! Ultimately managers felt a total loss of confidence in their ability to improve service enough in their stores to be identifiable and appreciated by the customer.

Boche understood she had to change the situation dramatically. Her first action was to go on the road to dismantle the existing system. She realized that Toys "R" Us needed to find out what its customers *really* wanted. While the issues being measured might have made sense in 1992 (when all of the studies were initiated), their current relevance needed to be reassessed. Boche needed to find out whether the issues were still relevant and whether service was in fact key to the company's business.

Concurrent with her investigation of customers' needs was the need to educate her "internal customers" concerning how each of the studies was intended to be used. Boche went around the country to store directors conducting meetings to educate them about service as both an art and a science and to teach them what these imperfect measurement instruments could and couldn't do for them.

Fixing a Broken Toy

Convinced that Toys "R" Us needed a different process for tracking its delight-producing capabilities, Boche began laying a foundation during a year of extensive site visits, both with the field and with the corporate-office staff. Her message? "We're probably going to have to make some changes." At the same time, she alerted her current vendors, telling them she was convinced she was going to have to make substantial changes. Boche openly admitted she didn't know what she would decide to do going forward. She checked all of the existing vendors' contracts. Her diligence was based in part on preparing for change and in part because she didn't at that point have a clear vision of the future.

Boche spent twelve months learning as much as she could about the current technology and thinking in the world of customer satisfaction measurement. She attended a number of seminars and took every cold call she received from research companies. She invited countless firms to come in and make presentations. She charged each potential supplier with two questions: If she were to stop what she was doing and start fresh in 1999, what would they advise Toys "R" Us to do? How would they advise approaching the changeover?

Boche listened to as many people as she could for weeks on end and started to weed some out. She based some of the eliminations on "people considerations"—could she work with them and how they were organized? How the potential vendors were internally structured was an important consideration for Boche, who considers herself a very hands-on person. She didn't want to have to go through countless layers in an organization to get to those who were conducting her research and preparing her reports. Boche felt "siloed" firms imposed a degree of difficulty in working with them that was not appropriate at a time when she needed a close relationship with a vendor in order to forge a new vision.

She narrowed down her potential partners to a small number of companies that she liked in terms of their presentations and their demonstrated understanding of the company's needs. One had even done some prior work for Toys "R" Us and came in with specific recommendations. Ultimately, one company offered an exploratory phase that it agreed to conduct as a stand-alone project—other companies had insisted on forming a structured relationship first. Without a clear understanding of the nature of the challenge, Boche was reluctant to form a long-term partnership until she had a better idea of her entire needs.

The investigation stage included focus groups that were conducted among both customers and store associates. To assure geographic representation, the discussion groups were held in three major markets. Customers were pleased to participate and had no shortage of ideas and comments. They also had ideas of how to re-instill a pleasurable shopping experience for customers. They complained, however, that the company had lost its focus on the customer and was too tied up in procedures and operations.

Messages from customers and associates were surprisingly similar. All agreed on some basic tenets of good service. What Boche needed to do was to reconcile these issues into questions that could reasonably be asked of customers. She added the current questions for comparison and further consideration. This became one of the most grueling aspects of the makeover. Many issues were similar, yet they were slightly different. She ultimately created a list of four criteria that a question needed to follow to be considered for inclusion in the satisfaction survey:

1. Was the question single-minded in thought and meaning?

2. Was the question stated from the customer's point of view?

3. Was the issue controllable, and at what level (at the store level, or at the corporate level)?

4. Are there specific behaviors or actions that could be undertaken at the store level to resolve the issue?

The Discoveries

As a result of the exploratory work, fifteen different performance variables were identified that were believed to correlate with a delightful store visit. These variables were taken forward into a baseline measurement, conducted in November 1998.

A unique aspect of the measurement was that store register transactions were used to sample customers for inclusion in the survey. Within forty-eight hours of the purchase transaction, a telephone interview was conducted with the customer. Satisfaction ratings on each of the fifteen variables were the first items collected. Beyond the ratings, verbatim explanations were also recorded. The numerical ratings created a way to track progress, and the explanatory information would hopefully help store teams better understand customer issues and give them the ability to solve them quickly.

The initial baseline measurement helped Boche accomplish a number of things:

- It provided a benchmark measure of the status of customer delight at Toys "R" Us.
- It provided a baseline for each of the fifteen variables, helping to identify those that needed the most immediate improvement.
- It supported further statistical analysis to help determine the extent each variable was correlated with customers' overall level of satisfaction, helping to prioritize the variables.
- It helped to identify delight levels associated with each variable to be used to prioritize corporate spending.

The baseline also helped to validate the importance of the different variables that had been measured. Using a key-driver analysis, ratings of the fifteen variables were correlated with ratings of overall delight (as opposed to mere satisfaction) to determine those variables that were most closely associated with delight. Variables with the highest correlations are considered the most important, or key. Those areas that were relatively high in importance to delight but showed relatively low delight levels were identified as action priorities.

One of the most compelling findings to come from the baseline measure was a comparison of the spending by customers broken out by their level of satisfaction (dissatisfied, merely satisfied, and delighted). Delighted customers were spending significantly more money at Toys "R" Us each year than were those customers who were not delighted. On average, the dollar amount of this difference equated to one and a half more shopping visits per year per customer.

The ramifications for Toys "R" Us were astronomical. The company was able to provide store managers with a very concrete example of how much it is worth to them to create more delighted customers. This same understanding helped corporate management commit to the goal of creating customer delight as a sound financial business decision.

As a result of the baseline findings, the measurement process was extended into a continuous, monthly process. The keys to making the ongoing program workable would be threefold: making information available to store and district managers on a continuous basis, guaranteeing that the information reported was representative of the actual store performance, and helping store managers react constructively by implementing improvement programs. Toys "R" Us considered it especially important to have explanatory information available to the stores as well as the numerical ratings.

A system was devised whereby stores would receive monthly reports showing the ratings generated by each month's interviews. All of the verbatim comments were also forwarded to the stores. These comments were especially helpful to the management team in working out issues with the associates who were responsible for serving customers. The whole report process was packaged to be consistent with the goal of Toys "R" Us: to "create magic" in the stores in order to delight customers.

Creating Delight

Customer delight is part of a wide-reaching strategy to improve customers' overall shopping experience at Toys "R" Us. It represents the cornerstone in a strategy to have the right people, the right products, and the right price to exceed the expectations of customers. In a Knight Ridder/ Tribune Business news article, Toys 'R' Us CEO John Eyler notes, "The challenge at Toys 'R' Us is to build an excitement level, a service level, and a presentation level of product so that when there's no hot toy we have a good year, and when there is a hot toy, we have an outstanding year." To achieve these aims, Toys "R" Us initiated a company-wide effort to provide its store associates and managers with the necessary tools and training to focus on the drivers of customer delight.

- "Toys 'R' Us plans to launch its biggest customer service overhaul ever. . . . The initiative . . . is intended to rally Toys 'R' Us's 52,000 U.S. employees to change how they treat customers." —Associated Press, 1999

- "Delighted customers! Friendly sales help! Toys 'R' Us!" —Ellen Simon, *Newark Star Ledger*, 1999

- "The most crucial step in winning customers back [to Toys 'R' Us] is improving customer service." —Rachel Beck, *Dallas Morning News*, 1999

The customer delight research also revealed that store support issues from the corporate office frequently impacted customers' shopping experiences. For example, every month a large percentage of customers who actually make purchases at Toys "R" Us leave without all of the items that they had intended to buy. (This does not include those customers that leave without making any purchase.) The vast majority of these missed sales result from customers' belief that the items are out of stock. Not surprisingly, few of these customers are delighted with their overall shopping experience. From a simple economic perspective, this represented a tremendous loss in revenue. Assuming that only one-third of this loss was controllable, its value would be conservatively in the tens of millions (if not hundreds of millions) of dollars. Worse still, it kept customers from being delighted.

Based on these findings, Toys "R" Us instituted a feedback process to determine what items customers left without purchasing and the reasons they were not purchased. This information was separated into the appropriate merchandising category and supplied to the appropriate merchandising department so that action could be quickly taken to minimize missed sales of popular items.

Did It Pay Off?

It became clear that, for Toys "R" Us, it pays to improve customer service. Research had shown that delighted customers spend significantly more money on average than those who are merely satisfied. Furthermore, there are significant opportunities to improve customers' overall shopping experience in order to increase sales.

Improving service remains a strategic corporate objective at Toys "R" Us. The results from the customer delight research enable everyone to know where to focus their efforts. And the management team is totally committed to increasing sales by creating customer delight.

Sales have shown a corresponding increase as noted by the headline of a January 2001 *Wall Street Journal* article: "Toys 'R' Us Reports Strong Holiday Sales as Competition Struggles, Orders Layoffs." The article goes on to note the important role improved service played in the company's ability to regain market share. Notes John Taylor, an analyst with Arcadia Investment Corporation, "The company is turning around the perception that it's a tough place to shop. It was able to pull off the positive [same-store sales] despite challenges . . . including the lack of hot products, lousy weather," and tough market conditions.

Summary

Throughout the 1990s, Toys "R" Us watched its share of the toy market decline in the face of intense competition. In an effort to curb the erosion of its market share, the company began modernizing the layout of its stores.

Toys "R" Us had also developed a well-publicized reputation for poor service even while the company was spending millions of dollars to both measure and improve the customer's shopping experience. Year after year research was showing no improvement in customers' perceptions of their shopping experience.

To remedy the situation, Toys "R" Us essentially began anew in terms of determining what customers want and in developing new measures of customer satisfaction based on these determinations. The research found that customers who were delighted spent significantly more than those who were not delighted. In order to capitalize on those findings, a measurement process has been institutionalized that provides the information necessary for managers to impact sales by delighting customers.

10

The Case of Mercedes-Benz USA

The authors thank Mark Juron and Maura Gallagher, general manager and manager, respectively, of the Client Assistance Center at Mercedes-Benz USA, for joining them in discussing the challenges accruing to a high-visibility company focused on customer delight.

MERCEDES-BENZ USA has what is probably the finest customer-care facility and operating practice anywhere in the world. The Client Assistance Center (CAC) is a group within Mercedes-Benz USA entrusted with being the first point of contact for inbound interaction with clients. We interviewed Mark Juron, general manager, and Maura Gallagher, manager, of client care to find out how they had so successfully "sold in" a customer-care philosophy to their organization. Much to our surprise, there aren't any dramatic pay-back models justifying the expense of maintaining a separate facility that houses seventy-five or more people and operates twenty-four hours a day! In fact, the whole commitment is taken pretty much as a commonsense, common decency thing to do. Juron explains his philosophy:

153

We consider what we're doing here as a simple commitment to those people who buy our cars. But our commitment isn't motivated by the amount our customers have paid for their car. Personally, I think the person who buys a Ford Focus is just as deserving of the same level of client care as somebody who owns one of our Mercedes-Benz autos, because each buyer spends a relative percentage of his or her disposable income on the car. And, when you consider it, the individual buying a Focus is probably spending a larger percentage of his or her annual income than our owners spend on a Mercedes. So it's not about the overall price. When a customer buys an expensive anything it's not necessarily a rational decision; it's an emotional decision. . . . We said, the right product at the right price with the right pricing strategy, and everything else, just won't be enough, because there are lots of options out there. For us to keep them, our owners have to be able to say, "You know, I've got this relationship with this company Mercedes-Benz that's really delightful!"

The problem is, when you sit in a planning room or boardroom, you either get it or you don't. It is such a simple philosophy. . . . That's not to say you're going to build the perfect environment—the CAC isn't perfect. I mean, we have employees and clients just like everybody, and we have some clients with problems and some with unreasonable expectations. The Mercedes-Benz USA Client Assistance Center is here to try to find a way to resolve the problems, to manage processes, and to evolve to address the ever-changing expectations of our constituency. But it's such a simple philosophy: "I'm a client; know me as a client, know my 'touch points,' and deliver to me. That's my expectation."

The Company

Mercedes-Benz USA (MBUSA) is a wholly owned subsidiary of Daimler-Chrysler AG of Stuttgart, Germany. The company has marketed automobiles in the United States since 1965 (though Mercedes-Benz autos were privately imported into the United States beginning in 1952). The company markets its automobiles in the United States through a retailer network comprised of 314 Mercedes-Benz centers. In 1999 Mercedes-Benz became the bestselling luxury marque in the U.S. market, selling an impressive 189,437 cars and trucks.

The Vision Starts

In 1991 Mark Juron was managing the company's New York City dealership. In that year MBUSA undertook a project called CEP, or cost-efficiency project, under then Vice President of Finance Wolfgang Hartung. As a part of this project, Juron and his colleague Joe Eberhardt were selected to lead two groups: Juron lead the group on customer satisfaction and Eberhardt had the group dealing with the marketing area. The sole purpose was to review the monetary efficiencies of MBUSA's operations and how the company was dealing with its customers—were they meeting clients' expectations and doing so in the most efficient manner for everyone involved? At the time, the company believed it was offering the best-built car on the road, but it wasn't sure its customers' experiences were always of an equivalent quality. Juron recalls:

> We started strategically looking at the way we had aligned the organization and it became alarmingly apparent that we had done it very much on a silo mentality and very much with corporate agendas and efficiencies at the forefront, but we really hadn't looked at what the client's experiences were. So we reviewed a lot of the focus groups we were conducting at the time, we relooked at other information we had, and we interviewed people—dealers, customers, and our own colleagues. One of the astounding things that became very apparent early on was that the sum of the parts was not as great in value to clients as the individual parts or services that we offered our clients. So where a customer would have very good experience in roadside assistance, another might have a terrible experience with our surveys and follow-up, and yet another might have a very poor experience with literature fulfillment, whether it was brochures or a request for technical information, and others were having both good and bad experiences with Client Assistance.

What they found by mapping internal systems was, at best, a challenge for all involved. The unit had over eighty different toll-free telephone numbers, so that each communication effort could track its effectiveness by counting the calls it generated, and eleven different client databases. It had retained five vendors to run various parts of the customer-service offerings, and each vendor had its own, unique database of customers. Each database contained different information and none of them were compatible. All of these variations made it very difficult to respond to customers intelligently or immediately because there was no way of knowing if or when the customer might have previously contacted any one of the five vendors or what might have been done for them.

Intent on simplifying things and organizing them in a way that would facilitate customer interactions, Juron's and Eberhardt's two groups came to independent but remarkably similar conclusions. Both groups recognized the need to create a revolutionary new organization. While they had their own ideas about how to organize things, they also wanted to learn from the best, so team members started taking a look at the client- care landscape. They visited several different companies outside the automotive category to observe world-class customer operations. Among the companies they benchmarked were American Express's telephone centers, GE's Answer Center, and Dell computers.

They returned from their benchmarking visits believing they could truly innovate the automotive client-care experience. But it wouldn't be easy, maybe not even possible, unless they could centralize both the database and operations. They created a working document that described the potential organization's structure, established a required budget, and most importantly specified the type of database and application the new organization would need in order to operate effectively. They produced pro forma operating forecasts for the next five years, a five-year capital-investment plan, and an ROI calculation based on the teams' estimates of incremental sales from clients touched by the new higher-care process. Juron explains, "We went out and took a look at the current organization and tried to identify what we thought were strategic parts of the MBUSA organization that were situated elsewhere in different environments and silos and that needed to be aggregated, put together from our client's perspective."

They took a bold step, proposing that all of those functions that interacted with current clients be housed together in one unique Client Assistance Center. And they proposed bringing ownership for the conduct of those services (most of which had previously been farmed out) within MBUSA. The teams were encouraged by U.S. management's agreement with their plan and support for the investment it required. Central to the idea was the establishment of a unified database recording all interactions with MBUSA's clients, regardless of the source of the interactions. Not only would it be a major contributor to retention efforts, but it could also support data mining and other future opportunities. There was also a cost savings to be realized, but the calculated payback timeline was an unconvincing five years. Truly, underwriting the reorganization had to rest in a commitment to serve clients better and more personally and not in any cost-efficiency argument.

Over a 1991 breakfast meeting in Germany, Juron and Eberhardt's plan won formal corporate approval. Subsequent to the approval, Juron was asked if he would take ownership of the initiative. He agreed and left the retail world in December 1991.

Creating a Customer-Focused Support Center

Having received corporate approval, Juron and three colleagues set up operations in an eight-foot-by-ten-foot cubicle early in 1992. Juron recalls:

> All we had was the fifty- or sixty-page document [presented in Germany] and a basic conceptualization of what we could do. We had the departments to be assimilated spread around the organization, with each probably having absolutely no concept of what they might be getting themselves into. We lacked the comprehensive database we had specified, so we proceeded to go out and integrate the various eleven databases that already existed.

In retrospect, Juron believes this integration was one of the most important things he and his teammates did. They sat down with the staff of all the different areas and explored their needs, wants, and desires. Juron and his team then used this input as part of their mission: to fulfill their constituencies' expectations as primary to fulfilling the needs of MBUSA's clients.

Striving for Excellence

The CAC was opened on February 19, 1993, and in 1994 MBUSA launched a corporate repositioning and some further restructuring oriented to better serving customers. The goal of the restructuring was to transfer responsibility down to MBUSA market managers (executives in the field operating at the local level). No longer would these managers have to wait for headquarters to authorize an action or to review volumes of paperwork to get approval on even the most mundane requests. With the reorganization, market managers were empowered to make many more decisions at the local level. This, in turn, helped to reestablish the respect local dealers had for the market managers, because the managers were now the last word in any debate.

This change also expanded the ongoing commitment to customers with a more visible component of the corporate culture. Empowerment at the local level gave client care and the Client Assistance Center the legs to go forward with its mission quickly, satisfactorily, and in a manner in keeping with expectations of the client.

The Mercedes Experience

The next evolution of client care for Mercedes took place in the latter part of 1999, with the adoption and rollout of a formal commitment promising that:

- All Mercedes-Benz products will be integrated and coordinated to create a sense of unity for the brand.
- The Mercedes-Benz name will be made synonymous with exceptional service and an exceptional experience.
- The company will focus on the individual needs and desires of each client in a way that goes beyond his or her expectations.
- MB clients will know that the company values and respects them and that MB employees are always prepared to go out of their way for them.
- Mercedes-Benz people at every level will anticipate and respond to clients' needs and desires.
- MB will genuinely listen and respond to its clients' needs and requests.
- Mercedes-Benz will foster and enhance client communications through current and future technology.

Several aspects of this commitment make it a noteworthy statement among companies operating in the United States, especially those in the U.S. automotive market. First, the statement clearly identifies customers as the focal point of all corporate activities. (Those concerned with helping companies self-modify in order to adapt to the evolving needs and desires of their customers have advocated this positioning for some time.) Second, a specific level of client reaction is specified: the goal is not mere satisfaction but delight—the client's expectations are to be exceeded.

Terms Are Everything

To help implement the philosophy, Juron reasoned that he would need to properly position customers to gain them the stature and respect to which the company believed they were entitled. A task force was assembled to evaluate the evolution of the Mercedes-Benz environment and to create new labels that would convey the proper image. The first new label the task force decided on was that customers would be called "clients." Customer Listening Groups, established to explore reactions to these new terms, confirmed that Mercedes-Benz customers appreciated the term *client*, saying:

- The term conveys a sense of respect, suggesting a professional relationship between them and the company.
- It implies a continuing interaction lasting throughout the owner's lifetime, not just a "momentary flirtation" at the time of sale.
- It challenges dealers to make a commitment to their customers, endeavoring to grow a relationship with them over time.

These were all qualities that the task force had sought to evoke.

Regarding Mercedes-Benz's dealers, the task force implemented a similar change in terminology. This change was considered essential to help reverse the public sentiment toward car dealers. To hopefully elevate Mercedes-Benz dealers to even higher levels in the automotive business, the company wanted to avoid the term *car dealer*. It was decided that "retailer" would be the new label because it was not overly burdened with negative baggage. The company reasoned that the term *retailer* could be shaped to reflect exactly the perspective Mercedes-Benz wanted to accomplish.

Function Follows Form

Juron and his colleagues at the Client Assistance Center dedicated themselves to evolving their organization to even better support such lofty goals. Customer delight was the most basic goal. But how do you delight customers who, because of their affluence, can be thought of as relatively demanding and well-experienced? The solution MBUSA reached was to reorganize many of the service-support functions around the customer and to house them together in a group oriented to the customer. This group was named the Client Assistance Center. Juron became the first general manager of this totally unique organization within Mercedes-Benz USA. Many companies who strive for customer focus lack the structure to adequately communicate with and respond to customers. The establishment of the CAC by Mercedes-Benz was a prima facie commitment to customers that could not be disputed.

Initially the CAC reported to MBUSA's president/CEO, who helped in resolving some of the reorganizational issues stemming from the establishment of the department. Subsequently, the reporting line was changed so that the CAC reported to the vice president of client services.

The center includes five areas: Client Assistance, Roadside Assistance, Consumer Promotions, Client Survey and Follow-up, and Client Warranty Services. The common factor uniting all activities is that these are the departments within Mercedes-Benz that interact with prospects and clients. MBUSA has centralized all customer-retention activities in one main department and all reporting to one manager, Juron. This makes Mercedes-Benz and the CAC among only a few organizations in the United States to have strategically separated retention activities from advertising and sales (conquest activities). "We believe," Mark observes, "that our organization reflects the manner in which a client sees us, as an entity, and that retention activities are not separate nor unique from day-to-day interactions." As such, employees at the CAC are free to concentrate on doing things to make owning a Mercedes-Benz a truly memorable experience. The CAC is available twenty-four hours a day, seven days a week, every day of the year; customer dialogue is completely centralized here. Each of the three most visible areas have their own focal point:

• **Client Assistance:** This is the center for measuring the quality of each client's relationship with the company. Its objectives are to provide a mechanism and support structure to measure, analyze, and internally communicate client experiences with Mercedes-Benz products, services, and retailers to MBUSA and its retailers. In this way it serves as the voice of the client within the company. It regularly conducts customer satisfaction surveys with purchasers and owners of new and previously owned Mercedes-Benz cars. And, it follows up on survey contacts with a client, either by telephone or through an acknowledgment letter.

Client Assistance also handles incoming telephone, written, and Internet correspondence with clients, as well as sharing responsibility for information request calls that come in through MBUSA's TeleAid service.

• **Roadside Assistance:** This group supports emergency communications with Mercedes-Benz owners. The group handles:

- Twenty-four-hour roadside assistance
- Trip-routing assistance for motorcar journeys
- Contacts through TeleAid
- Fulfills Sign and Drive, a unique program established to cure the three biggest worries of road travel: out of gas, a dead battery, and a flat tire.

- **Consumer Promotions:** This group is responsible for responding to clients' requests for information about their current or future cars, selling Mercedes-branded merchandise, and fulfilling requests for technical information literature. This area also manages the processes involved in special events such as driving clinics, events staged in conjunction with local retailers, and factory visits.

Other services are currently under development to extend the offerings of the CAC.

The Database

The heart of the Client Assistance Center is the database. As Juron and his colleagues established the concept of CAC, the database, as well as the applications overlaying it, were their most important concern. Juron elaborates:

> I think underlying everything is that we understood very early on that what we were really building was a client database at the core, and that we were facilitating the building of that by placing applications out there that would satisfy the expressed needs, requests, and desires of our clients but which, at the same time, would gather priceless data for us. . . . It wasn't about anything else but the database. Our mantra was, "If you build the database, they will come."

The database Juron and his colleagues built was named FASTRACC. The name was a somewhat facetious acronym, standing for Finally A System That Records All Customer Contact. The goal was to consolidate all of the information that existed about customers across the Mercedes-Benz USA organization into just one central repository. According to Juron:

> We had eleven internal databases but none of them put [the information] together in a useful mosaic describing the relationship of the owner or driver of the vehicle with our organization. . . . Even more frustrating, we'd call a customer, we'd ask a question, and we didn't have a vision [from a strategic standpoint] of who should be there to follow up when the customer's answer wasn't favorable. So we called and we asked, but we never called back again. We never knew what the ultimate resolution [to the situation] was. . . . But no one [in the company] ever saw any value to having [the information] all in one place. The clients saw the value to this because the clients said, "Know me. I want you to know me and my value and my relationship with you!" . . .

> When we stood back and looked at all the activities, each one of them unto
> itself was very good, but looking at the aggregate of all of them, [I thought],
> What are we doing?

Juron believes another decision has been critical to the ultimate success of the Client Assistance Center. There is a dedicated IT support staff within the CAC. Because the IT staff is a part of the CAC environment, it understands not only *how* to get something done, but *why* it needs to be done. Notes Juron, "I have absolutely no remorse to call at three o'clock in the morning to say, 'We have a problem!' It comes with the territory; if we have a problem, we are probably disappointing a client somewhere. Our belief is that sustaining a minor personal inconvenience is secondary to finding a replacement for a disappointed client."

The other extraordinary perspective is in the value accorded the client information stored in the database. Of course, it will never be shared with outside organizations. But also it will never be overwritten. According to Juron, "We make a commitment to our clients—we don't ever expire client information; we don't ever write over customer data. We may expire a client's relationship to a home or to a phone number or to an address, but the client will always be referenced in the permanent record associated with the car."

Making Systems Work

Juron and his colleagues were very diplomatic and strategic in the way they built their systems. They wanted to avoid corporate push-back later. Juron says he values the steps he and his team took to include two important groups in the planning: those who would use the systems and those who would work the systems. They wanted to establish a new culture within Mercedes-Benz. It was a top priority to see that all interests and values were incorporated. In particular they wanted each user to feel he or she had a vested interest in the process and in the CAC. To achieve that goal, Juron and his colleagues made it clear that, if people were willing to take the time to give their input, the IT infrastructure would be created the way they wanted it. Juron and his team also made a point to gather input from people who were joining the CAC from various other departments. Their involvement ranged from picking the furniture to designing the look of the work areas. All of these little things turned out to be of great importance in the building of the new culture at the CAC.

Juron also looked for the right people. He hoped to create what he describes as a rebellious culture. In fact, the spirit of CAC is captured in a slogan on the wall outside his office: "Challenge everything." His favorite questions to ask a candidate when recruiting early staff members were, Do you think the company is doing well? Do you think we should continue to market as we are, or not? Do you want to put your career on the line to try something new and radical, which, if it doesn't work, could mean we'll all be gone? He sees the role of CAC as challenging the Mercedes-Benz organization, its departments, the production and design of the automobiles, and anything else that could be challenged in manner or perspective from the client's viewpoint to continue to improve the Mercedes-Benz processes, products, and environment.

The Client Care Center

Good customer relationship management (CRM) systems incorporate two types of interaction, reactive and proactive. Most businesses today understand the value of reacting to customer feedback. With the current proliferation of Internet "suck-sites," the organization that doesn't allow unhappy customers to vent directly to it is probably inviting a customer-relations nightmare. But less widely held is the commitment to good proactive activities. Customer satisfaction surveys are the most obvious example. But not all survey systems are equally sensitive to customer needs nor do all include the same level of responsiveness.

Maura Gallagher, manager of client advocacy, describes her department as composed of two activities:

• **Client Survey and Follow-Up:** "Their real mission is to follow up with clients who have completed IBS [Initial Buyer] or SES [Service Experience] surveys, and either 1) help resolve issues that may have arisen during the acquisition or servicing experience or 2) delve more deeply into the feedback that the clients have provided us, trying to extract tips for future practices; to really gather more in-depth data than our client may have provided."

• **Client Care:** "This group oversees the conduct and utilization of the satisfaction program. Our primary job, what we spend 90 percent of our time doing, is administering the program—developing measurement and reporting tools that can provide ever more detailed feedback on our clients' experiences with purchasing, servicing, and owning a Mercedes-Benz. With the remaining 10 percent of our time we develop best practices, for both our retailers and our in-field executives."

Establishing Monitoring Systems

The satisfaction measurement program that Juron and Gallagher put into place is a very ambitious one. Rather than perpetuate programs of the rank-and-file car companies, they set out to redefine how customer satisfaction could be measured while also strengthening the communication ties between the client and Mercedes-Benz. In doing so, they reasoned, they would increase the bonds of the customer with the company, lengthening the lifetimes of customers and their value. They wanted all of their questionnaires and communications to be:

- Supportive of the Mercedes brand
- Highly personalized to the individual client, demonstrating the perceived value of the client and the resulting respect
- Customized to the particular Mercedes-Benz line and model the client is driving

Juron and Gallagher knew they would need a very detailed and accurate client base to drive such personalization and customization. Fortunately, FASTRACC offered all of the information that was necessary. Gallagher was able to draw from FASTRACC to provide the information required for the creation of highly customized interviews. The remaining problem was finding a partner to oversee the program in the fashion Mercedes wished. When the company identified a firm that placed the same importance on the cachet with which satisfaction measures were conducted as Mercedes desired, the program was turned over to that supplier.

The program consists of two questionnaires: one for the buying experience and one for the service experience. These two questionnaires are sent to each client. The buying experience questionnaire is sent within two weeks of the purchase and the service experience questionnaire within two weeks of each warranty servicing. The questionnaires are conspicuously identified as Mercedes-Benz and arrive in a very stylish mailing package. Besides the questionnaire, the package contains a personalized letter from the general manager of the CAC and a business reply envelope. Within the four-page questionnaire, twenty or more customizations are made, rendering the questionnaire a completely personalized message. The client's particular Mercedes is identified and the selling or servicing retailer is mentioned by name. In addition, the client is asked about his or her preferences for the mode of future correspondence. Mail, telephone (with choice of weekdays, weekends, and specific times), and Internet are all offered as possible media. It is Gallagher's intention to path future communications to each client according to their expressed desires.

Another unique aspect of the process they designed is the numerous opportunities offered to clients to respond in an open-ended fashion, telling the company anything they want Mercedes-Benz to hear. (Far too many satisfaction programs ask only what the sponsoring company wants to hear, providing no opportunity for the customer to tell what's on his or her mind.) In all, each of the two questionnaires offers five or six different areas in which clients can express themselves.

Client response to this personalized treatment has been rewarding. Almost two-thirds of all Mercedes-Benz owners respond to the buying experience questionnaire! This compares very impressively to the 20 percent to 30 percent response rates of the more conventional, noncustomized satisfaction programs other automotive manufacturers administer.

Responding to Client Feedback

The problem with many satisfaction-improvement programs is that they're all measurement with little or no power or method by which to actually improve products or service processes. In addition, while most programs collect information, few provide any response or remedy to participating customers. Juron and Gallagher didn't want to add their program to such company. They dedicated themselves to seeing to it that all comments from their clients would be reviewed, and where possible, clients would be contacted to have their issues discussed and resolved. Gallagher considers the competitive strengths of her program to be this interactiveness.

The two most impressive aspects, according to Gallagher, are the personalized service provided to both retailers and clients and the attentive follow-up. Gallagher explains:

> Every one of us answers the phone calls! We all return phone calls. And we'll delve deeper into an issue if our retailer or client wants us to. . . . I think clients are always surprised that we really do read *every* survey. It's not me

> personally sitting and reading every survey, but someone at CAC is going to read what each of our clients has said.

And, she believes the conduct and "look and feel" of her program is more in keeping with the world of Mercedes-Benz.

> Our program is a little classier than others; it's what you might expect from Mercedes-Benz, and that's important. Some of the other manufacturers' satisfaction programs don't go to the trouble we do to personalize our communications and then follow up and acknowledge clients' participation.

Acknowledging Compliments and Complaints

Offering clients the opportunity to provide ratings and to offer comments to the company would certainly be destructive if there were no process for following up on the information and requests offered. Because Juron supervises all five areas in the Client Assistance Center, any questionnaires that contain comments or questions that require follow-up are routed through the Client Assistance Center. Here, a Mercedes-Benz Client Assistance Correspondent takes ownership of the client's issue and places a call directly to the client to discuss the situation.

Incorporating Information Gathered

Gallagher is passionate about the results of her surveys. She believes:

> Information for information's sake is worthless. The only reason we should ask a client to spend time completing one of our questionnaires is if I honestly know it will get acted on, that the information learned will stimulate review of current procedures and trigger some improvement effort.

Constant Evolution

One of the more challenging aspects of the Mercedes-Benz CRM program is its inability to rest. Gallagher is constantly engaged in conversations with clients on how to improve the program from their perspective and with retailers to see how the program's findings can be made more useful. Gallagher admits, "One of the hallmarks of a good program is that it should never sit still, so today I'm considering how to use the Internet to make our program more client-friendly and how to use it to provide customized results for retailers on a continuing basis." Her goals for the future of her program are threefold:

1. Better anticipating major problems as well as the conditions of individual clients

2. Using all of her tools to strengthen the relationship Mercedes-Benz has with each client

3. Making the wealth of information her unit collects more accessible throughout the company for the benefit of more activities and more departments

Modeling the Relationship

When a company begins to understand what its customers want and expect, it can shape its marketing and other contact programs to more completely satisfy these desires. Mercedes-Benz has a campaign model that is driven by the date of a car's purchase. The model, shared by the local retailer and Mercedes-Benz USA, specifies what activities should happen and when. The program includes a welcome kit, the various questionnaires distributed throughout the lifetime of ownership, anniversary cards for the car, birthday cards for clients, and mileage awards celebrating the car's miles on the road (100,000; 200,000; and 500,000).

Did It Pay Off?

Today the Mercedes-Benz USA Client Assistance Center handles about 1.6 million telephone calls a year. The center has won numerous awards. Throughout the MBUSA organization there is an unspoken yet believed commitment to clients. Juron says, "You can question payback on our center and you can ask, How much? But you should also consider our understanding of our clients' emotional commitment to our brand and then ask, How could we not?"

Recognizing the value of tangible proof, Gallagher and Juron understand the importance of accountability; they know their management expects periodic review of departmental efforts. A second, perhaps even more compelling motivation exists for monitoring the payback of client relationships. Mercedes-Benz retailers, the company's main interface with clients, benefit from compelling evidence about the value of investing in and cultivating clients' delight.

So exactly how beneficial is a delighted customer to Mercedes-Benz? Figure 10.1 shows the value of delighting a client for a retailer. The data in these charts were taken from clients' expressed attitudes, collected in the MBUSA client relationship management program. (Within a year Gallagher's team will have a sufficient number of repurchase records to validate satisfaction with actual purchase data. In place of those records, repurchase intentions have been used in the current analysis.)

In Figure 10.1, Part A, the likelihood that a client who is dissatisfied with the service he or she has received at a retailer will rebuy or re-lease from that same retailer is only 10 percent! Those are odds of 10 to 1 against repurchase! Part B shows that mere satisfaction doesn't pay off that well either. There's only a 29 percent likelihood of rebuy or re-lease among merely satisfied clients. On the other hand, Part C, shows the likelihood of a delighted client rebuying or re-leasing is an astounding 86 percent—almost the converse of dissatisfied customers!

Beyond these very compelling attitudes, perhaps the greatest testimony to MBUSA's commitment to delighting its clients is its ability to show clients that MBUSA really knows them and thereby appreciates their loyalty. Juron describes how the program can neutralize a client's momentary anger:

> When we get a client who wants to speak with me, I always look through our database to find out what we know about him or her. Then in the telephone conversation, after the client has gone through the initial issue that he or she wants to speak with me about, I spend some time just going over what we know about that client. I have yet to have anybody who, having heard all the information we've collected about him or her, doesn't truly change his or her tone. . . . If an organization has gone to the effort to learn about you and has invested the wherewithal to do it, then I would suggest that the organization is conveying the importance of their relationship with you. That's not to suggest that we always come to total agreement on how to resolve a client's issue. But I believe in all of our interactions with clients (both those totally delighted and those with some issues), as an organization, we put our best efforts into maintaining a good relationship with them.

The Future and Delight

Juron believes he knows the future and why his mission and that of the Client Assistance Center is so important for Mercedes-Benz USA. He believes that with clients' rising expectations, the capabilities of the Internet, and other current and future technological innovations impacting the

Figure 10.1 *The Impact of Delight on Repurchase Intentions*

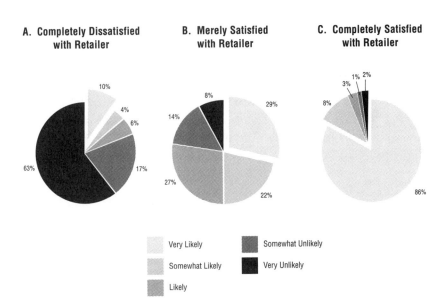

automobile business, price is no longer the key reason to do business with a company. Juron argues that the concentric circle of client expectations, needs, wants, desires, and values is going to be what takes the place of price as the leading factor. Differentiation of a product or service, beyond better pricing, is what will make the difference in profitability and success. Juron says, "Sure, you'll differentiate yourself with product; you'll also differentiate yourself with capabilities and values. But I think you'll differentiate yourself most with relationships and by making the relationship not just satisfactory but delightful!"

Summary

All too often companies set goals or objectives that their current organizational structure either fails to facilitate or actively inhibits. It is to the credit of Mercedes-Benz USA and its parent company that, when it decided to align itself more completely with its customers, it didn't simply stop at the words. Instead, it recognized the importance of creating an organization that would structurally support and facilitate the goal.

The Mercedes-Benz USA Client Assistance Center is a truly unique facility. It unites all of those corporate functions that interact with current customers, tearing down the walled silos so typical of modern corporations' numerous departments.

Beyond the mere organizational statement made by the center, the company's databases, which store knowledge about its clients and track interactions with them, are also integrated within the center. This makes it possible for any MBUSA representative to talk intelligently and in an informed manner with any client. The center manifests to clients the company's goal, making owning a Mercedes-Benz a truly delightful experience.

11

The Delight Epiphany

PEOPLE HATE CHANGE and businesspeople are no exception. And so, when it comes time for an organization to face the need for change, it will rarely be welcomed. In the last few chapters we've reviewed how three companies braced for change and evolved into the customer delight–oriented position they hold today.

The Dimensions of Success

Whether or not a firm truly benefits from the customer delight principle depends a lot on how the principle is implemented. In Chapter 7 we identified key criteria gleaned from our observation of numerous delight-seeking companies. These criteria determine the success or failure of any delight initiative. These six key characteristics, along with essential questions they should answer, follow:

1. **The business environment.** What is the nature of the firm's competition and the industry it competes in? How unique are the firm's products or services?

2. **The precipitating conditions.** What triggered the commitment to customer delight?

3. The sponsorship and commitment. What level of management is the overt sponsor of the delight initiative? How committed is management and is this commitment broadly shared across the entire organization?

4. Program design. Were customer insights and preferences solicited and used in the design and justification of the program? Is the organizational structure flexible enough for modification or evolution to better accommodate the needs of the delight initiative?

5. Technological support. Are the firm's technological competencies and information systems being properly utilized?

6. The role/involvement of employees. Have employees been educated, trained, and motivated to support the program? Do they understand reasons for adopting the delight initiative? Do they feel they have been a part of its design and goals?

Four of the five companies we have profiled have succeeded as the result of customer delight. As you've reviewed the actions of all five companies, no doubt you have personally noted how each one measures up on these dimensions.

The Business Environment

Roche Diagnostics was attempting to compete in a mature, low-growth industry with a parity offering. No real opportunities existed for distinguishing itself in the service it was providing. Carlo Medici determined that a delightful level of servicing could be the quickest opportunity to turn his company around. The industry was so mature, so staid, that no one had even considered they could excite customers with delightful service.

In quite the opposite direction, FedEx Custom Critical found that the dynamic growth of its industry had caused it to lose some of its unique servicing that its customers had come to expect. R. Bruce Simpson recognized that and was able to turn the tides by reintroducing personalized customer service as a distinguishing characteristic.

The Uniqueness of the Product or Service

Of our examples, Toys "R" Us best exemplifies a company that lost its uniqueness because of the entry of other, nonhistorical competitors, including Wal-Mart and Target. Toys "R" Us is currently attempting to regain its stature by teaming its assortment of products with the expertise of its staff to truly create and deliver customer delight.

What Triggered the Commitment to Customer Delight

The way companies latch on to customer delight can have a considerable impact on the success of a program. If customer delight is undertaken as the flavor of the month, it is likely to be unsuccessful. But when a company, like Roche Diagnostics, hangs its entire future on delighting customers, the effort is likely to be more genuine and therefore more successful.

Commitment from Management

Many companies have tried the customer delight principle. Some that we have worked with seemed to understand exactly what we were working for. But when it came time to implement, the companies that didn't have the organizational clout died for lack of a senior sponsor. That's why we believe that, to be truly successful, an organization's CEO must be turned on to customer delight. If the captain isn't behind the program, chances are neither will be the troops and neither will be a supporting budget.

Simpson of FedEx Custom Critical is exemplary in leading the passion for customer delight. He reads every questionnaire. His compensation, along with that of all other employees of the company, is based on customer satisfaction. And he speaks for it: "The most important component of our strategy for our core business, today and for the future, has to be to meet the expectations of perfection of our customers. Our strategy is to absolutely delight our customers!"

Carlo Medici certainly demonstrated his personal commitment when he admonished his management team by saying, "There is nothing more important than meeting the demands of our customers and deciding what to do to improve our level of satisfaction with this company!"

It would be difficult for an employee of any of these companies to question the sincerity of the commitment to customer delight. These CEOs and senior managers live the message, they don't just talk it!

Where or How Customers Are Positioned

In Chapter 6 we argued, as many have recently done, that to truly serve one's customers by understanding and anticipating their needs, the customer must be placed at the very center of the organization. That means organizing around the customer. But most companies become fairly rigid in their structure and they are reluctant to forgo the traditional departments established by "industry decree." The thought of adopting some new organizational structure that would better meet customers' needs is truly frightening.

Feargal Quinn, an Irish businessman and CEO of the national supermarket chain Superquinn, tells a compelling story dealing with organizational structure and how it manifests itself within an organization:

> We had just opened one of our newest stores. I was visiting to see how things were getting on when I was approached by the new store's manager. "Oh, Mr. Quinn, Mr. Quinn, this is a terrible situation!" he complained. "What do you mean?" I asked. "Well," said he, "the store's layout is all wrong! They've placed my office right over there, smack in the middle of the store, where all of our customers can see me. I can't get anything done. I've spent the last two days doing nothing but talking to our customers, answering their questions, listening to their complaints!" I looked him straight in the eyes and said, "Ahh, but that's the point, exactly!"

In this same vein, MBUSA turned itself inside out structurally in order to unite the various contact points customers had with it. In doing so, the company was able to better manage customers' needs and interactions. But it took the foresight of a group of Young Turks within to sound the alarm and wage the campaign for change.

The Firm's Technological Competencies and Information Systems

Business is about people, but with today's technology we can better serve an increasing number of clients if we use technological tools to help us maintain the familiarity and personalization they are looking for. Kenneth L. Roberts, to stress the importance of people at First American, was filmed in front of computers saying, "We're not about computers; we're about personal relationships." First American underutilized technology thinking it strategically inappropriate. Unfortunately they overlooked the benefits of technology. Computers could have assisted them in first identifying their high-value customers and then tracking the needs of this profit-giving group.

As customer intimacy and respect is adopted as a way of becoming more relevant to one's customers, technology will have to be harnessed to assist in the customization. But that doesn't mean an impersonal conduct of business—anything but! Actively listening to customers and being able to process and manipulate what they say can be a very compelling report to operational levels within a company. That means transcribing or digitally recording what customers say in telephone or personal interviews. Then, this information is sorted and organized by department or by product. The voice of the customer is hard to argue with.

Who Are the Employees Who Will Implement Delight?

Customer delight is a spiritual business. It takes people who are believers, who accept the strategic advantages of customer delight and are committed to helping achieve it. However, in today's labor market, as we observed in Chapter 5, finding dedicated employees is becoming more and more difficult. This shortage makes customer delight a more challenging goal and suggests that, while more than one firm may attempt to deliver it, not all will be successful.

After one of Carlo Medici's first meetings at Roche Diagnostics, about one-third of his technical force resigned. They didn't like the sounds of a changing culture and weren't emotionally prepared to buy in. "You have to be ready to take a hard stance and accept some issues in the short term. But you hire the right caliber of people who are committed to 'fixing' the customer and the machine," says Medici.

Accountability

Medici noted that "customer delight is a winning strategy, but it needs to be accompanied with your value proposition." In other words, customers are going to make tradeoffs between the delightfulness of the experience and the price they pay. For this reason, spending to create delight should be treated like any other resource-allocation decision. Customer delight should be expected to produce revenues that are greater than the costs.

Be it FedEx Custom Critical, Roche Diagnostic Systems, Toys "R" Us, or Mercedes-Benz USA, all committed substantial resources to the pursuit of delighted customers. These were not, however, blind investments with merely hoped-for outcomes.

As FedEx Custom Critical was implementing its Customer Assistance Teams (CATs), the company carefully tracked its success. It took the company three years to fully implement CAT, but early on it was apparent that the program would be a success. Notes Simpson, "We had measures in place to gauge customer satisfaction, and we found that the customers and the drivers were more satisfied with CAT than with the system it replaced."

At Roche Diagnostic Systems, one of the three main considerations for proposing and implementing improvements was available resources, given the company's highly volatile financial situation at the time. Furthermore, change was part of an overall strategic plan, the Challenge to Change, which had specific financial objectives for measuring success.

At Toys "R" Us, customers' spending levels were broken out by satisfaction level. This breakdown showed that delighted customers were spending significantly more money at Toys "R" Us each year than were customers who were not delighted. The financial ramifications helped corporate management commit to customer delight as a sound financial business decision.

Lavish spending may produce delighted customers, but without financial accountability, shareholders will be less than pleased. Ultimately, the justification for the effort must be its connection to the bottom line.

Scope

A word about who you should target to delight. You don't want to keep all of your customers. The fact is, many businesses fail by trying too hard to serve the wrong customers! You also want your efforts to delight to be paid back. To accomplish these goals requires carefully segmenting your customer base, identifying your high-value customers, and then shaping your delight strategies to meet their needs first and foremost.

Creating Delight

We've learned there is no one way to create delight, no magic formula, no three-step progression or pyramid. Creating delight for your customers first requires knowing and eliminating their points of pain, and then listening to their desires.

But listening must be done strategically. Customers must be coached to not only describe the things they like but also how important these things are or might be to them if offered. Prioritization will help you create delight through cost-efficient endeavors of only the most relevant activities.

Delight also comes from creative inspiration: the jovialness of a Southwest Airlines flight attendant; a warm cookie upon check-in at a Double Tree Inn; special seating at concerts or shows for American Express card holders. But delight doesn't have to come from extras or gimmicks. Just plain doing a job right the first time can be an exceptional experience in today's harried world. As Mark Juron of MBUSA observed, "It's about time, stupid!"

The best way to create delight is to gather as much information as you can about your customers. Then conduct some "ideation sessions"— brainstorming groups to help create "wild and wacky" ideas. Include your management, your frontline employees, even some of your customers. Tell them your goal, then turn them loose. Let them speculate on procedures and products that could delight your customers.

Also observe other organizations in other industries. Shamelessly borrow their good ideas and methods. Most of all, try to have fun as you build a delightful experience for your customers. Toys "R" Us found it useful to stage company-wide "Magic Moment" events to demonstrate to its associates that serving and delighting customers could actually be a very enjoyable and rewarding activity in and of itself.

Your First Steps

Beginning a customer delight strategy can be a very rewarding effort. It is the proverbial win-win situation. Your customers win because they're delighted. Your employees win because delivering delight is certainly more pleasant than delivering pain. And the firm wins because delighted customers come back and bring their friends. And employees who interact with delighted customers are more likely to remain in your labor force, which all-in-all means greater profitability!

W. Edwards Deming, father of the quality movement, really understood the marketplace and our avocation of customer delight when he observed, "It will not suffice to have customers that are merely satisfied!" We would add, they must be delighted!

References

Chapter 1

Adamson, J. Douglas (1991). "Quality Is America's Greatest Challenge," *Bank Marketing.* 23 (December): 44.

Anderson, Eugene W., Claes Fornell, and Donald R. Lehmann (1994). "Customer Satisfaction, Market Share, and Profitability: Findings from Sweden," *Journal of Marketing.* 58 (July): 53–66.

Anderson, Eugene W., Claes Fornell, and Roland T. Rust (1997). "Customer Satisfaction, Productivity, and Profitability: Differences Between Goods and Services," *Marketing Science.* (2): 129–145.

Anderson, Eugene W., and Vikas Mittal (2000). "Strengthening the Satisfaction-Profit Chain," *Journal of Service Research.* (November).

Bank Letter (1991). "Individual Bank Strategies: First American Pushes for Cost Containment," *Bank Letter.* (October 14): 7.

Bank Marketing (1992). "Service Quality Resource: BMA National Service Quality Study Zeroes In on News Bankers Can Use," *Bank Marketing.* (March): 37–38.

Bolton, Ruth N. (1998). "A Dynamic Model of the Duration of the Customer's Relationship with a Continuous Service Provider: The Role of Satisfaction," *Marketing Science.* 17 (1): 45–65.

Business Wire (1998). "Fears of Overbuilding Are Overblown, Lodging Research Network Says," *Business Wire.* (July 6).

———— (1998). "Hotel Industry Sees Best Financial Performance in Years, but Customer Satisfaction Is at Five-Year Low," *Business Wire.* (July 8).

Calvert, Jerry (1990). "Quality Customer Service: A Strategic Marketing Weapon for High Performance Banking," *IIE Solutions.* 22 (November): 54–57.

Cline, Kenneth (1992). "Nashville's First American on Rise: But Bottorff Says Expansion Ambitions Are Limited," *American Banker.* 157 (October 2): 2.

Colby, Mary (1992). "Quality Service Manager: A New Strategic Direction for the '90s," *Bank Marketing.* (April): 28.

Council on Financial Competition (1987). "Retail Excellence." Volume 1 of *Service Quality.* (October): 3.

DuBose, Jane Gibbs (1990). "Banker Used to Being in Public Eye," *Nashville Banner.* (May 30): B1.

Evans, Judith (1998). "Customers Rap U.S. Hotels for Slipshod Service as Rates Rise," *International Herald Tribune.* 11.

Fasig, Lisa Biank (1995). "Big Returns Come to Small Package: Roberts Express Stands Tall by Being Small," *Small Business News* (Akron). 4 (May): 26.

George, Richard J., and John L. Stanton (1997). *Delight Me.* Atlantic City, NJ: Raphel Publishing.

Harrow, Victoria Reynolds (1999). "King of the Road," *Inside Business.* 1 (November).

Higgins, Kevin T. (1997). "The Long Haul," *Marketing Management.* 6 (Fall): 4–7.

Jones, Terril Yue (2000). "Firestone CEO Suddenly Finds Himself at Center of the Storm; Profile: Masatoshi Ono Searches for Answers as Howl Over Defective Tires Threatens to Spin Out of Control, *The Los Angeles Times.* (August 30): 1.

Keates, Nancy (2000). "Luxury for Lilliputians: How Small Can Hotel Rooms Get?" *Wall Street Journal.* W1.

Keel, Beverly (1990). "Roberts Victim of Circumstance, Leaders Say," *Nashville Banner.* (May 30): B1.

Langdon, Jerry (1998). "Hotel Guest Concerns," *Gannett News Service.* (September 10).

Lunt, Penny (1992). "Just What, Exactly, Is Quality Service?" *ABA Banking Journal.* 84 (June): 78.

Mittal, Vikas, and Wagner Kamakura (2000). "Satisfaction, Repurchase Intention, and Repurchase Behavior: Investigating the Moderating Effect of Customer Characteristics," *Journal of Marketing Research.* (November).

Pickard, Jack (1993). "Motivate Employees to Delight Customers," *Transportation and Distribution.* 34 (July): 48.

PR Newswire (2000). "StrataSource's Money-Back Guarantee Raises the Bar for Customer Satisfaction; New Program Replaces Service Industry SLAs," *PR Newswire.* (August 30).

Quality Focus Institute Staff (1991). "Deciding Where to Start on Service Quality," *Bank Marketing.* (April): 50–52.

Royal, Weld F. (1995). "Keep Them Coming Back: Satisfying Customers (The Personal Touch)," *Sales and Marketing Management.* 147 (September): 51.

Salter, Chuck (1998). "Roberts Rules the Road," *Fast Company.* 17 (September): 114.

Sherborne, Robert (1990). "Roberts Ousted After Long, Hard Thought," *The Tennessean.* (June 3): 1A.

Silber, Kenneth (1989). "Bank Hands Out Report Cards," *Bank Systems and Technology.* 26 (November): 26.

United States Banker (1991). "Outsourcing Plus: International Business Machines Corp. Provides Outsourcing Services to First American National Bank," *United States Banker.* 101 (October): 88.

Warner, Melanie (2000). "Confessions of a Control Freak," *Fortune.* (September 4): 130–140.

Chapter 2

Bonsignore, Michael (1996). "How Total Quality Became a Framework for Honeywell," *Minneapolis Star Tribune.* (April 15): 3D.

Boulding, William, et al. (1993). "A Dynamic Process Model of Service Quality," *Journal of Marketing Research.* 30 (February): 7–27.

Brownlee, Shannon, et al. (1997). "Lies Parents Tell Themselves About Why They Work," *U.S. News & World Report.* 122 (May 12): 58.

Chandler, Colby H. (1989). "Quality: Beyond Customer Satisfaction," *Quality Progress.* 22 (February): 30–32.

Communication World (1995). "An interview with Jerre Stead, EXCEL award recipient. (Legent Corp. CEO)(Interview)," *Communication World.* 12 (June 16): 49.

Deming, W. Edwards (1986). *Out of the Crisis.* Cambridge, MA: MIT Center for Advanced Engineering Study.

Howard, John A., and Jagdish N. Sheth (1969). *The Theory of Buyer Behavior.* New York: John Wiley & Sons.

Incantalupo, Tom (1990). "The Quality Quandary," *Newsday.* 50 (May 13): 52.

Jones, Thomas O., and W. Earl Sasser Jr. (1995). "Why Satisfied Customers Defect," *Harvard Business Review.* 73 (November/December): 88–99.

Miller, John A. (1977). "Studying Satisfaction, Modifying Models, Eliciting Expectations, Posing Problems, and Making Meaningful Measurement," *Conceptualization and Measurement of Consumer Satisfaction and Dissatisfaction*, H. Keith Hunt, ed. Cambridge, MA: Marketing Science Institute, 72–91.

Oliver, Richard L. (1993). "Processing of the Satisfaction Response in Consumption: A Suggested Framework and Research Propositions," *Journal of Consumer Satisfaction, Dissatisfaction and Complaining Behavior.* 2: 1–16.

——— (1997). *Satisfaction: A Behavioral Perspective on the Consumer.* New York: McGraw-Hill Irwin.

Oliver, Richard L., Roland T. Rust, and Sajeev Varki (1997). "Customer Delight: Foundations, Findings, and Managerial Insight," *Journal of Retailing.* 7 (3): 311–336.

Rust, Roland T., Anthony J. Zahorik, and Timothy L. Keiningham (1994). *Return on Quality: Measuring the Financial Impact of Your Company's Quest for Quality.* New York: McGraw-Hill Irwin.

Seattle Times (1990). "U.S. Car Makers Struggle to Regain Loyalty of Auto-Buying Public," *Seattle Times.* (June 3): E4.

Swan, John E., and Linda Jones Combs (1976). "Product Performance and Consumer Satisfaction: A New Concept," *Journal of Marketing.* 40 (2): 25–33.

Chapter 3

Kaplan, Robert S., and David P. Norton (1996). *The Balanced Score-card*. Boston: Harvard Business School Press.

Semon, Thomas T. (1998). "Consider a Statistical *In*significance Test," *Marketing News*. 33 (February 1): 9.

Chapter 4

Anderson, Eugene W. (1994). "Cross-Category Variation in Customer Satisfaction and Retention," *Marketing Letters*. 5 (Winter): 19–30.

Anderson, Eugene W., Claes Fornell, and Roland T. Rust (1997). "Customer Satisfaction, Productivity, and Profitability: Differences Between Goods and Services," *Marketing Science*. 16 (2): 129–145.

Anderson, Eugene W., and Mary W. Sullivan (1993). "The Antecedents and Consequences of Customer Satisfaction for Firms," *Marketing Science*. 12 (Spring): 125–143.

Carberry, Charles M. (1999). "Napoleonic History Flows in 'Lost Fleet'," *USA Today*. (September 16): 08D.

The Columbia Encyclopedia (1993). "Napoleon I," *The Columbia Encyclopedia,* Fifth Edition. (January 1).

Danaher, Peter J. (1998). "Customer Heterogeneity in Service Management," *Journal of Service Research*. 1 (2): 129–139.

Garbarino, E., and M. S. Johnson (1999). "The Different Roles of Satisfaction, Trust, and Commitment in Customer Relationships," *Journal of Marketing*. 63 (2): 70–87.

Kano, Noriaki, et al. (1996). "Attractive Quality and Must Be Quality," *The Best on Quality,* John D. Hromi, ed. International Academy for Quality, Volume 7, Milwaukee, WI: Quality Press.

Kekre, S., M. S. Krishnan, and K. Srinivasan (1995). "Drivers of Customer Satisfaction for Software Products: Implications for Design and Support Service," *Management Science*. 41 (9): 1456–1470.

Life (1997). "1799: Stone Code," *Life* (Millennium Supplement). 20 (Fall): 17.

Mattila, Anna S. (1999). "The Role of Culture in the Service Evalua-tion Process," *Journal of Service Research*. 1(3): 250–261.

Mittal, Vikas, and Wagner Kamakura (2000). "Satisfaction, Repurchase Intention, and Repurchase Behavior: Investigating the Moderating Effect of Customer Characteristics," *Journal of Marketing Research*. (November).

Mittal, Vikas, Pankaj Kumar, and Michael Tsiros (1999). "Attribute-Level Performance, Satisfaction, and Behavioral Intentions over Time: A Consumption System Approach," *Journal of Marketing*. 88–101.

Mittal, Vikas, William T. Ross, and Patrick M. Baldasare (1998). "The Asymmetric Impact of Negative and Positive Attribute-Level Performance on Overall Satisfaction and Repurchase Intentions," *Journal of Marketing*. 62 (1): 33–47.

Oliver, Richard L. (1996). *Satisfaction: A Behavioral Perspective on the Consumer*. New York: McGraw-Hill.

Ralston, R. W. (1996). "Model Maps Out Sure Path to Growth in Marketplace," *Marketing News*. 30 (May 20).

Reichheld, F. F., and W. E. Sasser (1990). "Zero Defections: Quality Comes to Services," *Harvard Business Review*. 68 (September/October): 105–111.

Roy, Soumya (1999). *Case of a Pharmaceutical Company: Using Business Outcomes Modeling to Build Customer Loyalty*. Princeton, New Jersey: The Gallup Consulting Group.

Srinivasan, N., and B. T. Ratchford (1991). "An Empirical Test of a Model of External Search for Automobiles," *Journal of Consumer Research*. 18 (September): 233–242.

Zahorik, Anthony J., and Roland T. Rust (1992). "Modeling the Impact of Service Quality on Profitability: A Review," *Advances in Service Marketing and Management*, T. Swartz, ed. Greenwich, CT: JAI Press, 247–276.

Chapter 5

Anderson, Eugene W., Claes Fornell, and Roland T. Rust (1997). "Customer Satisfaction, Productivity, and Profitability: Differences Between Goods and Services," *Marketing Science*. 16 (2): 129–145.

Benkhoff, Birgit (1997). "Ignoring Commitment Is Costly: New Approaches Establish the Missing Link Between Commitment and Performance," *Human Relations*. 5 (6): 701–726.

Buckingham, Marcus, and Curt Coffman (1999). *First, Break All the Rules: What the World's Greatest Managers Do Differently*. New York: Simon and Schuster.

Farwell, Bryon (1984). *The Gurkhas*. New York: W. W. Norton.

Garvin, David A. (1995). "Leveraging Processes for Strategic Advantage," *Harvard Business Review*. (September/October): 76.

Hallowell, Roger, and Leonard A. Schlesinger (2000). "The Service Profit Chain: Intellectual Roots, Current Realities, and Future Prospects," *Handbook of Services Marketing and Management*, Teresa A. Schwartz and Dawn Iacobucci, eds. Thousand Oaks, CA: Sage Publications.

Heskett, James L., Leonard A. Schlesinger, and W. Earl Sasser (1997). *The Service Profit Chain*. New York: The Free Press.

Leibovich, Mark (1999). "At Amazon.com, Service Workers Without a Smile," *The Washington Post*. (November 11): A1.

Mathieu, John E., and D. Zajac (1990). "A Review and Meta-Analysis of the Antecedents, Correlates, and Consequences of Organizational Commitment and Job Performance: It's the Nature of the Commitment That Counts," *Psychological Bulletin*. 108 (2): 184.

Mowday, Richard T., Layman W. Porter, and Richard M. Steers (1982). *Employee Organization Linkages*. New York: Academic Press.

Pfau, Bruce (2000). "Employee Commitment Goes Hand-in-Hand with Shareholder Value," *St. Louis Post-Dispatch*. (February 1): B1.

Smith, E. D. (1998). *Valour: A History of the Gurkhas*. New York: The Overlook Press.

Rust, Roland T., Anthony J. Zahorik, and Timothy L. Keiningham (1994). *Return on Quality*. New York: McGraw-Hill Irwin.

——— (1996). *Service Marketing*. New York: HarperCollins.

Spector, Robert (2000). The Nordstrom Way (keynote speech). Presentation given to the 11th Annual MICS Conference by the Institute for International Research.

Spector, Robert, and Patrick D. McCarthy (1995). *The Nordstrom Way*. New York: John Wiley and Sons.

Wiener, J., and J. C. Mowen (1985). "Source Credibility: On the Independent Effects of Trust and Expertise," *Advances in Consumer Research,* Association for Consumer Research, R. Lintz, ed. 13: 306–310.

Chapter 7

Trinklein, Mike, and Steve Boettcher, creators of *The Oregon Trail* (documentary video). http://cwis.isu.edu/~trinmich/Discoverers.html.

U.S. Department of the Interior (1990). "Chapter 4: The Mountain Man as Explorer, U.S. History," *Exploring the Great American West.* (September 1).

Chapter 9

Associated Press (1999). "Patrons R Us? Big Overhaul for Toy Seller," *Newsday.* (June 12): A23.

Beck, Rachel (1999). "Service Game: Toys 'R' Us Plans Disney-Inspired Makeover of Customer Satisfaction," *The Dallas Morning News.* (June 12): 12F.

Brooker, Katrina (1999). "Toys Were Us," *Fortune.* (September 27): 145–148.

Covert, James (2001). "Toys 'R' Us Sees 3% Same-Store Sales Growth in 2001," *Dow Jones Newswire.* (March 7).

Drug Store News (2000). "Lebhar-Friedman Honors 'Best of Century' Retailers," *Drug Store News.* 22 (April 24): 4.

Klebnikov, Paul (1998). "Trouble in Toyland," *Forbes.* (June 1): 56–60.

Queenan, Joe (1998). "Take Me to Your Loss Leader," *Chief Executive.* (July/August): 68.

Simon, Ellen (1999). "Toys 'R' Us Talking Up New Concept: Friendly Help Is Key to Chain's Effort to Regain No. 1 Status," *Newark Star Ledger.* (June 16).

———— (2000). "New Toys 'R' Us CEO Is Committed to Improving Operations, Confidence," *Knight Ridder/Tribune Business News.*

Wall Street Journal (2001). "Toys 'R' Us Posts 6.8% Profit Gain, Credits Solid Online Holiday Sales," WSJ.com (March 7).

Chapter 11

Quinn, Feargal (1993). *Crowning the Customer: How to Become Customer-Driven.* Dublin: O'Brien Press.

Index

The American Marketing Association is the world's largest and most comprehensive professional association of marketers. With over 45,000 members, the AMA has more than 500 chapters throughout North America. The AMA sponsors 25 major conferences per year, covering topics ranging from the latest trends in customer satisfaction measurement to business-to-business and service marketing, attitude research and sales promotion, and publishes nine major marketing publications.

For further information on the American Marketing Association, call toll free at 800-AMA-1150.

Or write to:

The American Marketing Association
311 South Wacker Drive
Suite 5800
Chicago, IL 60606-2266
Fax: 800-950-0872
URL: http://www.ama.org